Right on the Money

Financial Advice for Tough Times

PAT ROBERTSON

New York Boston Nashville

FaithWords
Hachette Book Group
237 Park Avenue
New York, NY 10017

Visit our Web site at www.faithwords.com.

Printed in the United States of America

First Edition: May 2009

10 9 8 7 6 5 4 3 2

FaithWords is a division of Hachette Book Group, Inc.
The FaithWords name and logo are trademarks of
Hachette Book Group, Inc.

Library of Congress Cataloging-in-Publication Data
Robertson, Pat.
  Right on the money : financial advice for tough times / Pat Robertson.
    p. cm.
  Includes index.
  ISBN 978-0-446-54958-5
  1. Finance, Personal—Religious aspects—Christianity.   2. Finance, Personal—United States.   I. Title.
  HG179.R5472 2009
  332.02400973—dc22
                                                        2009003246

Contents

Acknowledgments

Right on the Money is my nineteenth book, and I must say that my experience with Michelle Rapkin, the Executive Editor of Hachette, has been the most agreeable that I have experienced from any publisher. I am deeply grateful to Michelle for her hard work in bringing this book to fruition, despite personal sorrows in her own life during this project.

I also want to thank my secretary, G. G. Conklin, for her work in typing and organizing the manuscript.

And, in particular, I would like to acknowledge my Vice President, Edie Wasserberg, who has been a great encouragement in the production of television features on finances for my program, *The 700 Club.*

Beyond this, my deepest thanks and appreciation to Jeff Opdyke whose brilliant analysis of investment philosophy has played a key role in this book, which I hope will prove successful.

The Big Picture

A reporter asked John D. Rockefeller, the founder of Standard Oil and at that time the richest man in the world, how much money was enough.

Rockefeller is reported to have replied, "Just a little bit more."

He was right. Wealth cannot satisfy. Therefore, to those in the money game there is always a drive for more...a little bit more...then a little bit more. We constantly torment ourselves in a never-ending quest for that which money and possessions can never provide—inner peace, fulfillment, happiness.

Some years ago, I was conversing with a prominent real estate agent. He said almost wistfully, "If I could only have one million dollars, my problems would be over."

"You poor fool," I thought to myself, "if you only knew how ridiculous that statement is."

First, when finance is measured in billions and trillions, a million is really not that much money in this day. Second, it cannot possibly bring lasting satisfaction. Third, it introduces a level of complexity into an average person's life for which he or she is not truly ready. Fourth, it merely replaces a longing for money with the fear of losing it. Fifth, it induces greed.

Greed—the Lust of "Wanting It Now"

Look at the financial chaos that human greed has produced. It is perfectly natural and proper for a family to desire adequate shelter, and then, in time, to want to move up to more spacious and pleasant surroundings…all in the appropriate time when income and investments make it possible for a growing family to enjoy the home of their dreams. That is not greed. Greed is like lust. One definition of lust is "wanting it now."

The Recent "Big Picture"

During the past decade, politicians wanted votes from citizens who were provided with ridiculous opportunities for home ownership. Widespread greed took over. Home builders wanted generous profits from massive housing developments. Mortgage brokers carved for themselves a lucrative niche from the housing bonanza. Then the Wall Street investment houses joined in to create and then to inflate the value of housing-backed securities.

At the heart of the rapidly expanding bubble were average Americans who succumbed to greed and bought houses they could not possibly afford, financed by variable-rate mortgages offered by unscrupulous brokers who either required no valid supporting documentation or supported an application with outright lies.

This cornucopia was too much for the Wall Street investment houses to resist. They took the government-blessed mortgages, then packaged them together as support for billions of dollars' worth of high-yield paper called "collateralized debt obligations." These questionable securities were submitted to the major ratings agencies, which promptly declared them triple A—suitable for investment by municipalities, banks, trust funds, and school endowments. Then, like a terrible plague, billions of these toxic things were sold (at a healthy profit) all over the world.

The day of reckoning came in 2007 when millions of new homeowners (and speculators) realized that they could not possibly afford the monthly interest payments that were due on their home loans after the low-cost teaser rates on their mortgages were reset to prevailing market rates.

There quickly followed a wave of foreclosures, abandoned houses, and bankruptcies. Suddenly it was clear that the emperor had no clothes. Venerable banks and investment houses that were gorged with "collateralized debt obligations" had no concept what these things were now worth. Were they to be valued twenty cents on the dollar, thirty cents, fifty cents, or zero? No one knew precisely the value of billions of dollars' worth of mortgage-backed securities because no market existed on which they traded.

Soon credit markets seized up because banks could no longer prove their solvency. Then the Securities and Exchange Commission exacerbated the problem by insisting on so-called "mark to market accounting." This meant that financial institutions were being forced by arbitrary accounting rules to raise billions of dollars in fresh capital or be declared insolvent.

The stock markets around the world dropped precipitously—businesses were unable to find credit. A potentially devastating depression was looming on the horizon.

The government acted swiftly. Ben Bernanke, the chairman of the Federal Reserve Board and a leading expert on the 1929 Depression, realized that this devastating period of our history was brought on after a stock market crash when the government raised taxes, adopted protectionist tariffs, and restricted money. He is known as "Helicopter Ben" for his statement that in order to forestall a future depression, the government will "throw money out of helicopters."

Throw money they did—a $700 billion "Troubled Asset Relief Plan"—$150 billion to insurance giant American International Group (AIG); $500 billion backing for commercial paper; $29 billion to guarantee the debts of Bear Stearns; $20 billion each to mortgage giants Fannie Mae and Freddie Mac; a $300 billion backstop for Citigroup; opening the Fed discount window for borrowings by investment banks; lowering the Fed funds rate (the rate at which banks lend to each other) to 1 percent. According to Bloomberg, the sums put out in various rescue efforts total, as of this writing, an incredible $12.5 trillion. Because of this the larger national monetary base has grown an astounding 38 percent in one year, unprecedented in our history.

Why the Authorities Are Taking Such Drastic Action

A much more ominous cloud is looming ahead. During the heady days of the real estate bubble, lenders attempted to protect themselves with insurance policies against defaults. This practice quickly morphed into a bucket shop operation in which insurers were writing policies for those who had no financial interest in the transactions. Imagine that you or your bank obtains an insurance policy against a default on your mortgage. Now imagine that each of the neighbors on your block obtains a similar policy on your mortgage. These neighbors have no financial interest in your house, but are simply gambling that you will or won't default on your mortgage or that your house will or will not burn down. The name given to the exotic variations of this theme is **credit default swaps,** and by their use certain banks were able to leverage their core capital up to forty times. The notational value of outstanding credit default swaps is $50 trillion. Small wonder the government could not permit the world's largest insurer, which had written the most default policies, to fail.

As enormous as the credit default swaps market is, there exists an unregulated market almost fourteen times larger. Billionaire investor Warren Buffet calls the components of this market "financial weapons of mass destruction." They are called **derivatives**.

A derivative is a bet on the price of anything—oil, gas, precious metals, grain. Wall Street has created synthetic derivatives based on mathematical theories involving market trends, volatility, the interplay of currencies, and so on. Although few people really understand the risks of these things, they are dangerous enough for one twenty-something junior rogue trader in derivatives to bring down England's Barings Bank, a venerable institution that had been in business since the time of the Napoleonic Wars.

Imagine an unregulated market, trading contracts that only the most sophisticated understood, that has notational value approaching $700 trillion—larger than the gross national product of the entire world!

The treasury regulators don't mention the derivatives market, but they understand that if one or more of the major players defaults, the resulting chaos could plunge the entire world into financial hell.

Absent some apocalypse, the smart money is betting that the torrent of government money will ultimately bring on rampaging inflation. At this moment, the markets have pummeled crude oil, natural gas, industrial metals, and agricultural commodities. Even gold, which is normally resilient in times of financial turmoil, is down at the time of this writing 25 percent below its 2008 high of $1,000 per ounce.

Spending by the United States government, along with massive fiscal stimulus from China, Japan, the United Kingdom, and other advanced nations must, of necessity, be inflationary. This means that in 2009, absent a deflationary collapse, the price of commodities and commodity-related stocks should be higher. I would not be surprised if gold made a dramatic upward move.

Some commentators put it as high as $1,800 an ounce. (Of course, there's no guarantee this will happen.) Crude oil prices in an inflationary environment should crest beyond $100 a barrel, while at the same time the world's stock markets would be moving neither up nor down...the so-called "hockey stick" recovery.

Project Your Own Hopes and Dreams

This book is about you and your financial decisions. Money, after all, is a means to an end, not an end in itself. Your ultimate success and happiness will not be measured by how much money you have at death, but by how much good you have done with your money while you are alive. In your planning and budgeting, always put first what you want to do for others—for your church or synagogue, for the poor, for the relief of human suffering, to provide education and a better life for those less fortunate. Few of the great pioneers of industry set out to accumulate money. Instead, almost all desired to build an enterprise that would create products or techniques that would enrich the lives of their fellow man.

For you, money could be a provision for a comfortable retirement when leaving the workforce. People save for the college education of their children. Others set as a goal a particular sum of money in savings. How much do you want to accumulate for a home, education, retirement, or current living? Perhaps you want to start a business. Plan out what you want and where you would like to be at forty, or fifty, or sixty. It's never too late to start, but it's a great deal easier if you start young.

In a world where emerging nations like China, Brazil, India, the United Arab Emirates, and even Russia are rapidly accumulating wealth, and using that wealth to consume parts of the U.S. economy, money is no longer something that just happens to you. You have to be savvy enough to understand what today's events mean to your wallet, whether that involves protecting yourself from financial tragedy or benefiting from the sweeping changes rapidly redefining the world's financial landscape. It means putting your money to work smartly and not simply shrugging your shoulders because you don't know what to do or where to look for the answer. Ignorance is no excuse in a court of law, nor is it one that has ever served finances well.

Had homeowners understood the risks of the nontraditional mortgages they pursued during the housing boom of the mid-2000s, banks ultimately wouldn't have been overwhelmed by an abundance of bad loans that led to record numbers of foreclosures and the collapse of housing prices around the country. The economy wouldn't have suffered so badly and the financial institutions that went bankrupt would probably still be around today.

These troubles all stem from greed, but insufficient knowledge about personal finances is what turns those troubles into disaster.

That is why I've written this book. America needs a refresher course on the characteristics that built this country into a financial power, one reliant upon itself, extending its hand to help others, where planning for tomorrow—not living for the moment—was a virtue. Families today need a better grasp on their money and a better understanding that mastery of their own personal finances can be key to a happier, more secure life. The Book of Proverbs speaks to this exquisitely: "The plans of the diligent lead surely to advantage. But everyone who is hasty comes surely to poverty."

Diligent planning is a cornerstone for successfully managing personal finances. Become a planner, one diligent enough to save without succumbing to the temptation of unnecessary spending; one who budgets and plans for the future without being forever sidetracked by the wants of the moment; one who is unburdened by the stresses of debt and knows that, no matter what ill wind might blow, his or her finances will weather the inevitable storms.

None of what you're about to read is difficult. You need never fully understand the operation of "variable rate mortgages," "credit default swaps," or "derivatives." The path to financial self-sufficiency isn't marked by MBAs from the Wharton School or complex analytical equations or secret handshakes. Neither money nor personal finance is a club open only to those of a select caste.

The knowledge is available to anyone wise enough to seek it.

Right on the Money

1

Why Aren't I Rich?

This question, which many ask, could just as easily be why aren't I tall? Or, maybe, why aren't I beautiful?

Of course there's no way to answer such subjective questions, because the fact is you might well be tall or beautiful or, even, rich. As we all know, beauty—and in this case, height and wealth—are in the eye of the beholder. What's short to some might be tall to others. What's rich to some isn't to others.

Everyone has a different operational definition of what it means to be rich. The chief executive of a company listed in the Standard & Poor's 500-stock index might feel rich earning $14.2 million a year, the average pay for that group in 2007, according to the Corporate Library, a corporate-governance firm. He can buy a beach-front mansion in Palm Beach, Florida, and can travel the world with his family in first class without ever considering the cost. Then again, the plumber in Akron, Ohio, earning $75,000 annually might feel just as wealthy because he owes nothing on his home, can afford two weeks' vacation with his family every summer at a cabin in Michigan's Upper Peninsula and, as his own boss, can set his work schedule around his son's hockey tournaments. He has all the joy he seeks in life.

We all measure wealth using different yardsticks. There's no way to address the question "Why aren't I rich?" by offering a canned answer.

Secrets to Wealth

The principles discussed in this section will bring you remarkable financial and spiritual happiness. The first secret is what I call the **Law of Use**. Most of you have heard the biblical parable of the talents (Matthew 25:14-30). It is a story of three sums of money (called talents) given to three servants by a nobleman. One received ten talents, another two talents, and another one talent. The first two servants began diligently investing the money assigned to them. They were entrepreneurs—wise investors. After a period of time, both had doubled their employer's money. On his return, he praised them for their diligence, and then gave them a dramatically expanded scope of responsibility.

The third employee was afraid of potential losses. He buried his one talent in a non-interest-bearing account with no potential for gain. When the nobleman called for his account, he proudly showed off his one talent, admitted his fear of loss, and declared over time he had lost nothing. The nobleman exploded in anger. "You wicked and slothful servant, you should have at least earned interest on my money."

Then, amazingly, the nobleman shouted, "Take the talent from him and give it to the one who has ten talents, for unto him who uses well what he has, more will be given; and he who does not use what he has, even what he thinks he has will be taken away from him."

This Law of Use is the universal law of human growth and development. It is without question the foundational law of financial growth. In times of steady inflation, the "wicked and slothful servant" leaves his money in a non-interest-bearing checking account, which over time, because of inflation, gradually becomes worthless. Or he is afraid of the complexity of investing and, thereby, spends all of his money on current consumption, entering retirement a virtual ward of the government.

A corollary to the Law of Use which leads to significant wealth is compounding, whose technical name is the "exponential curve." Consider this incredible wealth generator. The key is the rule of 72. Wealth doubles exponentially by the amount of compound interest divided into 72. In other words, if you're able to receive 20% annual compounding of principal and interest, your wealth will double in just 3.6 years. At the same rate, that amount doubles again in 3.6 years, and again, and again, and again. Although it seems hard to believe, this doubling will inexorably produce vast wealth so much so that it seems virtually miraculous. That's why Baron Rothschild called compound interest "the eighth wonder of the world."

When I was chairman of a good-sized public company, there were two numbers I focused on—compound annual growth rate of sales and the compound annual growth rate of profits. We targeted the top line at 30 percent growth, the bottom line at 20 percent growth. This is the key for a little company to become a big company. Stock of such a growing company ordinarily commands a premium.

The law of compounding can also work against us. Debt at a compound can destroy the finances of an individual, a company, or a nation. It is impossible to escape the fundamental laws of the universe.

A final secret is having the **blessing of God on your finances.** That secret is activated by your giving. In my financial planning, giving takes precedence. When that is true, the other steps to financial prosperity set forth in the later pages of this book flow together. They become dramatically alive whether in good times or bad. We start with a tithe.

A tithe is a tenth of a person's income. Tithing to God's work is fundamental to the teaching of Christianity and Judaism. In the Old Testament, there was not one tithe but three. Therefore, I determined to give away not 10 percent of my income, but 30 percent.

For me, that part of my budget was given priority over everything else.

Remarkably, the U.S. Tax Code allows for deductions from taxable income for gifts to charity not at 10 percent, not at 30 percent, but at a whopping 50 percent!

The biblical obligation comes with a promise. The Book of Deuteronomy states, "Be sure to set aside a tenth of all that your fields produce each...so that the Lord your God may bless you in all the work of your hands" (Deut. 14:23ff). In the book of the Prophet Malachi, there is this incredible statement: "Test me in this...and see if I will not throw open the floodgates of heaven and pour out so much blessing that you will not have room enough for it" (New International Version).

That extraordinary promise was fulfilled in my life. In 1959, I arrived in Portsmouth, Virginia, with a wife, three children, no job, and a total of seventy dollars in my pocket. I was on a mission to purchase a rundown UHF television station and take the airwaves from the "Prince of the Power of the Air" and give them to the "Prince of Peace." I received a contribution of thirty-five dollars and with it formed a nonprofit corporation called the Christian Broadcasting Network, Inc. (CBN). The early days were difficult. Total income in year one was $8,000. In year two, it was $20,000. In those early years, I never asked anyone for anything for myself. My family and I lived simply, yet we never lacked. In time, CBN grew, and by 1975 we owned television stations in Norfolk, Atlanta, Dallas, and Boston and were broadcasting across America.

As I gave, I prospered personally, but CBN (after very rapid expansion) was struggling with $500,000 in debt. In a memorable meeting at the old Adolphus Hotel in Dallas in 1973, the CBN board of directors determined that, despite our obligations, we would tithe our income to other ministries and other charitable endeavors. Then, indeed, the "floodgates of heaven" opened. In 1976, our total income jumped 250 percent over the previous year, and it grew dramatically every year thereafter. By 1986, our income was so large that the tithe on the amount—just the tithe—was sixteen times larger than the amount of our total income in 1973.

The story doesn't end there. In 1979, we established a small relief agency called Operation Blessing International Relief and Development, Inc., to receive a major portion of CBN's charitable giving. In the same year, we began the CBN Cable Network, which was renamed the Family Channel. The Family Channel became so successful that the IRS encouraged a spinoff into a separate company, International Family Entertainment, which we later took public on the New York Stock Exchange in a very successful IPO.

In less than five years, the Family Channel had attracted deep-pocketed suitors with offers too good to turn down. In bidding between News Corp and Disney, News Corp won with a bid of **one billion eight hundred twenty million dollars**. Indeed, the floodgates of heaven had opened, but that was not the end.

At the close of fiscal year 2008, CBN was sending programs in fifty languages to over 200 nations. It had built television studios in Manila, Jakarta, New Delhi, Hyderabad, Hong Kong, and Kiev.

Operation Blessing was distributing 100 million pounds of food and supplies each year to the poor of America, and was conducting medical missions and relief efforts all over the world at a total cumulative value of some $1.5 billion.

The combined annual income of CBN and Operation Blessing had reached $550 million. Again, consider this all started with God's promise and seventy dollars!

The Bible tells us that the generous person will be made

prosperous, but those who withhold more than is necessary will experience poverty. Generosity should be the foundation of your financial plan.

Proverbs 10:22 reads: The blessing of the LORD, it maketh rich (King James Version).

2

Why Do I Run Out of Money?

No matter how you measure "rich," success in attaining your definition of wealth comes from two basic factors—managing your financial life to a budget and keeping a tight rein on consumer debt.

Adhering to the principles of budgeting and controlling the urge to spend can play a major role in creating wealth. Combined, budgeting and debt management determine how much money you have for buying a house, for funneling some of your income into a retirement account, and for buying stocks, bonds, or mutual funds in an investment account. When you live according to your budget, you are living within your means, and when you control debt you are keeping yourself from the clutches of financial forces that can easily swamp your life. Both practices will help you fortify your finances against the bad times that can occur in families, in economies, or in financial markets. Budgets and debt controls will allow you to carve out part of your income for investment purposes, which is how families build financial security.

Every successful financial life begins with a budget. In good times, budgets give you the freedom to make spending decisions that enhance your life, improve your lifestyle, or allow you to prepare for the future. In bad times, they keep you true to your necessary expenses while highlighting the extraneous costs that you can cut to conserve capital.

Budgets are not evil creatures. They do not aim to keep you from spending your money on what makes you happy. They are not the equivalent of a monetary straitjacket that provides no wiggle room. Used properly, a budget can be enlightening and liberating. It can show you where you are spending too much on items that ultimately mean very little to you, and it can show you where you are spending too little on the things that mean the most to you. If your financial life feels like a path through the darkness, as many people feel theirs is, then a budget is the nightlight to show you the way.

Budget Basics: Fixed versus Discretionary Spending

Too often people structure their fixed costs with little regard to their discretionary spending. Then, they go about the month spending as they normally would on discretionary purchases, allowing their finances to suffer.

What I mean is this: People will buy more house than they can rightly afford, or will lease an expensive car they could not otherwise buy with conventional financing, and they do so looking at the individual cost in a vacuum. *I can afford that mortgage at $2,000 a month or that car lease at $600 a month,* they rationalize, *because that price is within the bounds of my monthly paycheck.* Yet they don't fully consider the impact such a fixed expense necessarily imposes on their discretionary spending every month. They don't consider all the meals they eat outside the home, all the clothes they buy, the movies they see, the concerts they attend, the books they buy. They sign on the dotted line for that mortgage or car lease and continue spending on daily life as they normally would, only to complain that they can never seem to get ahead. In the worst cases, such an unbalanced financial life falls into utter disarray and the only recourse is bankruptcy.

You have the power to prevent all of that before it's ever a threat by understanding your fixed costs and discretionary costs.

Fixed costs are fixed. They don't change from month to month, or if they do—as with utilities payments—the change is relatively marginal and within a general range. These are costs you have committed yourself to pay, and they must be paid at the risk of losing your home, being evicted from your apartment, losing your insurance coverage, having your car repossessed, or coming home one day to find the water, cable TV service, or electricity cut off.

Discretionary costs come at your discretion. They do not recur monthly, arising only when you do choose to spend. The size of the cost each month is directly related to how often you act on your impulse to buy whatever it is you covet at some particular moment. Controlling your discretionary spending is a key to gaining control over your financial life.

Basic Budgeting

That's where budgeting comes in. Budgeting is not a complicated task. It's not highbrow math and no MBA is required. You don't need spreadsheets, though you can use one if you want to speed up the process. You don't need computer budgeting programs. All you need is a desire to take control of your finances with a single piece of paper and something to write with.

Start with this very simple exercise. Write on any piece of paper every fixed expense you have. Start with your tithe, then include rent or mortgage, car payments, utilities, groceries, student loans, alimony/child support, childcare expenses, insurance payments (if you pay annually or quarterly, calculate the monthly cost), and any debt balances you have that require a monthly payment. Total those costs. They are your fixed expenses, the costs you are required to pay monthly.

Above that total, write your monthly, after-tax income, the

amount of money deposited into your checking account every month. Subtract the fixed costs from your income and what you have remaining is your discretionary dollars.

Knowing how much discretionary income you have is important because it allows you to determine how much money you can save every month—an absolute must if you ever hope to feel financially secure—and it provides you a high-water mark limiting the amount of money you can spend on consumer purchases.

Your discretionary income is all that you have to fund your wants for the month. Spend more than that, and you are digging yourself into a hole. Spend less, and you are building an ever-stronger fortification around your finances.

The Beauty of a Budget

Taking the time to define your discretionary income allows you to determine your wants. Those who complain that their income isn't sufficient to provide for the lifestyle they want, or who grouse about an inability to save because they're already struggling to makes ends meet, are really saying that they have no control over their discretionary spending, no financial self-restraint, and no compunctions about not budgeting. A budget is not telling you what you can and cannot buy. It's your discretionary income telling you that. You can buy whatever you determine is most important, so long as it fits within the confines of the discretionary income you have available in your budget every month. Your budget is nothing more than your road map—avoid it at your own peril.

If you determine your discretionary income isn't enough to let you live as you want, you have a few choices: You can find a higher-paying job; push for a raise at work; create added income through freelance opportunities or a part-time, at-home business; or—and this is more easily accomplished—restructure your fixed costs and, in particular, your discretionary costs to lessen their impact on your finances.

With fixed costs, you can refinance your mortgage to a lower rate, or downsize to a less-expensive house. You can rent a cheaper apartment. You can be more cost-conscious at the supermarket, trading premium brands for store brands in many cases, or buying your fruits and vegetables from a local greengrocer instead of the supermarket. You can buy regular gas instead of super premium. You can shop for more affordable insurance policies or cut out certain costs that you've committed yourself to but that don't provide a proportional benefit, such as premium cable channels you rarely watch or a mobile-phone plan that provides unlimited texting or data services that you could do without. Take the time to scrutinize your fixed costs and think about all the ways that you might trim a few dollars here and there.

Restructure Your Discretionary Spending

Over the course of several months, keep a journal that tracks your expenses every day. Whenever you spend any money—cash, check, or credit card—make note of it in your journal. Where are you really spending your money? You might instinctively think the bulk of your spending is on restaurant meals or, maybe, clothes. But when you see the numbers, you might discover you've actually spent an unusually large amount on soft drinks and snacks, or music downloads to your iPod, or just random, spur-of-the-moment purchases. That's the knowledge you need to redefine your finances. It is as important as the dollars themselves.

Seeing that you are spending excessively on certain items allows you to purposefully redirect your spending to that which is more important to you. That's as difficult as budgeting gets. You're not forcing yourself to live as a hermit; you're forcing your budget to serve your needs in smarter fashion. Knowledge of where your discretionary dollars go gives you the power to curtail what you define as wasteful spending so that you can reallocate those same dollars to whatever you define as productive spending. In effect, you are giving yourself a pay raise because your money is now stretching to better meet your needs.

Ultimately, an inability to live as you see fit isn't a matter of a paycheck that is too limiting. It's a matter of discretionary spending that is too haphazard, or of fixed costs that are beyond your true ability to pay. Gain control over those factors and you can build robust finances capable of withstanding the challenges that sometimes face the individual family, the community, or the broader economy.

Building Your Budget

This is actually the simple part of budgeting. All you really care about every month is your discretionary expenses, because on a month-to-month basis discretionary spending is the only spending that changes and, thus, the only spending you can manipulate.

In some instances, of course, your fixed costs will change in a given month. You might, for instance, pay off your house or car or some other debt, eliminating a fixed payment. You could move to a more costly or cheaper apartment, changing your monthly housing cost. You might lease or buy a new car, adding a mandatory payment. But those are relatively infrequent events, so you won't be changing those inputs on your budget all that often.

You will, however, change your discretionary spending, because your consumer-spending pattern is often different from one month to the next. This is where budgeting becomes liberating instead of taxing. When you finally realize you have the power to control where your money goes, you will see that a budget can help you achieve the lifestyle and financial security you seek.

Part of that security, by the way, is learning to routinely fund a savings account with some of your discretionary dollars. This is a must. Indeed, savings is the first expense that should come from your discretionary income stream, but I'll cover this more in a coming chapter.

Once you determine how many discretionary dollars you can spend each month (after subtracting an appropriate amount for savings), allocate the money to whatever you want to spend it on in the next thirty days. Where this money goes is entirely your choice. What do you want to spend your money on this month? A three-day vacation over the holiday that's coming at the end of the month? A new suit or a pair of shoes? Do you want to send money to an investment account, or donate to a local charity? How much do you want to spend on restaurant meals or lunchtime meals at work?

As you allocate these dollars, subtract them from your discretionary-income balance. When it reaches zero, you're done spending and you have a plan in front of you for exactly how the month will progress financially. Jigger the plan as much as is needed, moving dollars from one cost center to another to meet your wants. If you don't have enough money to pay for that three-day weekend, for instance, then trim costs that you don't mind forsaking. Bring your lunch to work instead of going out with the gang every day and allocate those savings to your vacation.

What you don't want to do is budget your discretionary dollars based on historical spending patterns as defined by some average of what you've typically spent on some category in the past year. That's budgeting through the rearview mirror, and the view you're seeing may not reflect the bend in the road in this month's pending spending. Historically, you might spend on average $300 a month at the supermarket, but this month you're planning a special gourmet get-together for twenty friends, a cost that by itself will likely exceed your average monthly supermarket bill. Yet penciling in

$300 for supermarket expenses in this case is clearly misleading and will cause you to blow your budget when the real costs come in closer to $600 while you continued to spend elsewhere in your budget as though all was normal.

Effective monthly budgeting is a dynamic, change-as-you-go process. When you know you're going to spend $300 on gourmet meal supplies, factor that into your budget and trim other costs accordingly. Cut other entertainment spending, like restaurant meals and movies for the current month. Delay until next month the clothes purchases you expected to make. Doing this frees up the money you need for the most important costs while reducing, delaying, or eliminating expenses you deem less pressing.

If you haven't realized yet my ultimate message, it's this: You have absolute control over your budget. Your budget is never in control of you. Those under the misguided perception that a budget prevents them from spending on what they want to buy do not understand that money isn't a force to reckon with but a tool to employ in your best interest. You are free every month to spend money in whatever way makes you happy, and you're free to alter your spending during the month to meet your changing needs.

The only chore is actually determining how you want to spend your money this month, so you don't run out of money.

3

Where Do I Get Credit
Where Credit Is Due?

America is awash in credit. Too much credit.

If you are an average American consumer, you likely have in your wallet at the moment four credit cards, according to a study by Experian, one of the big credit-reporting agencies. One in seven of you, the so-called heavy users, carry ten or more credit cards. In some parts of the Northeast, that rate is even higher. On those credit cards, there was a combined outstanding balance of nearly $1 trillion as of the middle of 2008, according to Federal Reserve statistics.

We are a nation that has been seduced by the pursuit of demonstrable affluence. Where once our national abundance reflected itself in a healthy bank balance, a strong savings ethic, and our role as creditor to the world, today we demonstrate our wealth by wearing it, driving it, living in it, or buying it—often on credit sucked into the United States from foreign countries that fund our extravagance with their savings. In the first 108 months of the twenty-first century, the U.S. personal savings rate nudged above 3 percent of income only five times. During the buying-and-lending orgy of 2005, 2006, and 2007, personal savings spent almost the entire period at or below 1 percent. For the forty years before that, our national savings ranged between 6.5 percent and 12 percent of our income.

Forget Prozac Nation of the 1990s. The new America—the one

of ever-larger houses, ever-bigger malls, ever-trendier clothes and gadgets and gizmos, and the ever-more-encumbering credit-card bills that ensue—has become Profligate Nation.

It shows in our national debt, which at more than $10 trillion at the end of September 2008 is the largest the world has ever known. It grows by the day by billions of dollars as leaders in Washington borrow incessantly to pay for underfunded federal programs and military misadventures and financial bailouts. With government as role model, and with a variety of economists supporting the ridiculous notion that "deficits don't matter," it's little wonder Americans continue to blindly bury themselves in debt.

Credit, and more specifically credit-card use, goes to the very heart of budgeting and, in particular, discretionary spending. Credit cards turn consumer purchases into a mindless game. When you spend real dollars, the paper in your wallet, you see the one-to-one impact on your spending decisions as your stack of greenbacks dwindles with every purchase. Clearly you reach a point where you recognize that the next purchase will totally deplete what you have in your wallet and you begin to more closely scrutinize your litany of wants.

Not so with credit cards.

When you regularly sign for your purchases during the month instead of paying with cash, you don't see this direct relationship between the spending and the whittling down of your resources. You aren't likely to remember every single transaction or the running tally of costs you've so far committed yourself to repaying. Your spending can easily sail well past your income. In colloquial terms, you've "blown your budget." Do that a few too many times and suddenly you find yourself under such a stressful load of debt that the mandated minimum payment might well at some point exceed your financial capabilities.

I'm not implying that credit cards are inherently evil. They're nothing more than a tool that, like a nail-gun, serves a useful purpose, but that can just as easily cause serious injury when misused. Misapplying your credit card means allowing your balance at the end of one month to roll over to the next. A balance is a clear sign that you have too much debt and an indication that you are living beyond your means. Though credit card companies will love you since you're paying them interest payments every month you allow this situation to exist, you're doing more to hurt your financial future than you are benefiting your present.

Some people will argue that a manageable level of debt is healthy, that all you're really doing when you charge a vacation or a new couch, or buy a bigger and better TV every few years, is pushing present-day costs into the future. In the future, these people argue, your income will be larger and you'll be able to erase today's debts with tomorrow's bigger dollars.

Maybe. But you are gambling. Such a scenario presumes a tomorrow that might not arrive as you optimistically envision. It presumes you never face a financial emergency and that you don't allow your credit-card balances to rise more quickly than you expected. I'm not a pessimist. But for the sake of your financial security someone has to be a realist. Bad economies happen. Bad health happens. Good companies are mismanaged and unsuspecting workers lose their careers. Any of these events and a hundred others can muss up all the best-laid plans, and what you're left with is a dwindling bank balance and a load of debt you can't escape.

Managing your credit and your credit card is the key here.

The Cardinal Rule of Credit Cards

Never carry a balance.

If you currently have a balance on your credit card, pay it off (and I'll tell you how to do so in a moment), and then don't accumulate another balance again. To be perfectly clear, what I'm saying is this: If you can't afford it, don't buy it. Savvy personal finance really is that easy, though consumers struggle with that dictate because easy credit means they can have everything they want, today, and worry about it off sometime in the future.

That's no way to structure your finances. If you have the money available, or will have it when your paycheck arrives, and you're relying on credit for convenience, fine. You'll pay off the debt at the end of the month and you're no worse off. But if you know going into the transaction that you will have to carry the cost from one month to the next, then clearly you cannot afford your want-of-the-moment. In this case, making the purchase is a bad decision.

Credit cards represent just about the most expensive money you will ever borrow outside of a loan shark. The only difference is that the credit-card company won't hunt you down and threaten to break your kneecaps if you don't repay by Friday. Instead, it will just ruin your credit score for a few years, making everything you buy on credit markedly more expensive, since current lenders will likely hike the interest rate of your existing credit cards and future lenders will impose higher rates on tomorrow's purchases to protect themselves against the credit risk you represent.

The average credit card in late 2008 charged an annual interest rate of between 13 percent and 14 percent on purchases. Some cards exceeded 20 percent. By comparison, the average car loan was about 6.5 percent through a bank, down near 0 percent for many automakers that provide financing to their customers. Home loans were somewhere in the 5.75 percent to 6.25 percent range for a thirty-year, fixed-rate mortgage. A lot of people, however, don't know what 20 percent really means to your wallet on a monthly basis. Nor do most consumers understand interest. They see a $1,000 balance and figure if they make that minimum twenty-five-dollar payment every month, they'll have the cost of that new TV knocked out in just over three years, just in time to replace it with a newer model.

Or not.

Go off and buy that TV for $1,000 on a credit card with a 20 percent annual interest rate, and then never use the card again and vow to simply make the minimum payments—twenty-five dollars a month—until its repaid. You will mail in your final payment nearly fifteen years later.

More shocking is the fact that over those nearly fifteen years, you will repay that original $1,000 loan, and an additional $1,465 in interest payments. Your 20 percent interest rates means you pay nearly 2.5 times the original cost of your TV. Given that fact, was carrying a balance really worth the true cost?

When you pay off your balance every month, the process works in your favor. You are using the credit-card company's money for free. You have access to their cash for one month without interest charges accruing, meaning your money can sit in the bank for those thirty days earning a small bit of interest for you. You certainly won't grow wealthy off such small interest payments, but you are assured of never having to pay a much larger interest payment to the credit-card company.

The Cardinal Rule of Credit Cards, Part II

Do not apply for more than two cards.

Do not apply for multiple credit cards and gasoline cards and branded store charge cards that promise you an immediate 10 percent savings for enrolling today. Lenders make obtaining a new piece of plastic easy and enticing. The applications arrive in the mail almost daily, or are displayed prominently at the checkout counter, or are eagerly hawked by checkout clerks when you pay for your purchases. The cards offer all manner of rebates and discounts and airline miles designed to make them seem like a deal you cannot pass up.

But the strategy of applying for multiple credit and charge

cards can be damaging to your wealth. At worst, you risk running up a cumulative, supersized balance, because the human mind works so well at compartmentalization and at fooling itself. You use the MasterCard for a while, for instance, and at some point during the month you hit a mental spending limit, that trigger in your brain that tells you you've accumulated enough debt on this one particular card because you don't want to be freaked out by a massive balance due when the bill arrives. Yet instead of halting your purchases on credit, you switch to the Visa or the American Express or the Discover card in your wallet and start racking up purchases on that card—then switch to a third card at some point for the same reason. You are compartmentalizing your purchases. Your brain is telling you that the balance on any one particular card is manageable, and you buy into the fallacy.

You're playing a mental shell game, though. Regardless of your financial gerrymandering, the fact is you must repay *all* the balances on *all* the cards. So what if your mental trigger is $1,000 a month—if you hit that trigger on three separate cards, you still owe $3,000 or more to creditors. If you can't repay that accumulated balance in full at the end of the month, you've hit the point at which so many consumers mark the descent into their own financial hell. More than likely, you'll repay what you can on each card, maybe even just the minimum due, and then start the same process over next month, ultimately growing a bigger and bigger balance on each card with each passing month. In playing this game, you are all but certain to lose, because at some point—and that point *always* arrives—you will reach a credit-card-company-imposed spending limit on one or more of your cards. What you're left with at that moment is the realization that you have no exit strategy, no idea how to repay $20,000, $30,000, maybe even $40,000 in credit-card debt. You ultimately can dig yourself out of this hole with great effort and sacrifice, but it will require time and determination. More on that in a moment.

Limiting your purchases to just a single, primary credit card goes a long way toward preventing this. The same mental trigger will warn you that you're approaching your spending cap for the month, but without multiple cards to fall back on you have no way to continue spending on credit.

Now, while I say you should limit spending to a single card, you should always have two credit cards available to you as a financial fail-safe. Keeping just one card risks technical snafus that can leave you hamstrung if your card is declined for some reason. Maybe you like the American Express card, but if some merchant does not accept AmEx, you may not be able to complete a necessary purchase. A second card used only as a backup can keep your financial life moving smoothly. But just to protect yourself from an overactive consumer gene, you might consider requesting a relatively low spending limit on this backup card. That way you can't ever charge a troublingly large balance.

The Best Credit Card

Everyone has individual needs and wants when it comes to credit cards. And credit cards these days come in so many different varieties that it's impossible as a consumer to keep track of all the permutations. The Internet, however, offers numerous resources to help with the legwork.

I would advise you not to simply sign up for any old credit card that happens to land in your mailbox, or to fill out an application you find as an insert in a magazine. Neither card might be right for you. Credit cards are not identical. Some offer low interest rates but charge high fees. Some have no annual fees but charge high interest rates. Some are aimed specifically at consumers with the strongest credit scores, others at consumers with impaired credit. You want a card that best addresses your specific situation.

(Continued)

Your best solution for finding the right card is online. Websites such as Bankrate.com and Creditcards.com are consumer-oriented sites that help you weed through thousands of competing credit cards to find those that offer the best options for your needs.

Both sites are free and are packed with consumer-oriented news, advice, and tools, including calculators to show you the true cost of paying the minimum balance due on your card or how much money you'd save by transferring your balance from one card to another.

4

How Do I Dig Myself Out of Debt?

Have you ever paid attention to the language associated with debt? People "get into debt" and then "struggle to get out of debt." The world once knew of "debtor's prison" for those who failed in that struggle. Consumers "drown in a sea of debt" and labor under "a mountain of debt." None of that imagery is pleasing.

Fact is, some debt is good. Some debt is bad. Good debt: a mortgage on an affordable house, since homeownership historically builds wealth, the housing crisis of 2007–8 aside. Good debt: a college education that opens the door to more lucrative or more fulfilling careers and better opportunities for you and your family. Good debt: a loan on an affordable car, since mobility, like a university degree, opens up opportunities not generally available if you are limited to public-transit routes. (This isn't necessarily the case in a place like Washington, D.C., New York City, and other communities with extensive subway and rail links.) These borrowings typically serve to improve your life and strengthen your finances.

Bad debt: consumer debt, such as the accumulated balances on your credit cards, or home-equity loans and lines of credit. These borrowings typically improve your lifestyle though they weaken your financial strength.

Luckily, bad debt is reversible.

How to Systematically Pay Off Your Creditors

From the outset, though, you have to be mentally committed to extinguishing your bad debt. Debt is as much a state of mind as it is a state of financial reality. Just as recovering alcoholics sometimes lapse into their habit and destroy all the progress they've made, debt-addicted consumers too often start on the path to financial redemption and get waylaid by negative thoughts and counterproductive actions. You can't do that. This exercise demands patience. You didn't build this pile of debt overnight, and you cannot expect to extinguish it overnight either.

Here's the game plan in a nutshell: You will limit your spending to a single credit card; you will cancel or put away most of your remaining cards; and you will begin to pay down your individual balances every month, concentrating your effort on the smallest balance first.

First Step

Determine which card you want to keep. My advice: Keep the card with the lowest interest rate, since that will keep your costs down during this debt-eradication process. But the decision is yours. You might want to keep the card that gives you airline miles or the one that contributes money to your child's 529 College Savings Plan. That's fine. Whatever you choose, this will be your primary credit card from here on out.

Second Step

Lighten the load in your wallet. Get rid of all the other cards you own except one backup card to use in the event your primary card is rejected for some reason. Any other card in your wallet goes away. Cancel those cards that already have a zero balance and stick those that don't in your family lockbox or safe-deposit box and leave them there. Once you've paid off one of those cards, cut it to shreds and call the card company to close the account. Warning: Do not rush to cancel each of the cards you'll no longer use. The longer you demonstrate your creditworthiness, the stronger your credit score. The credit card you've owned the longest helps establish your credit history. So the card you've had for the most years is beneficial. Consider using this one as your primary card or your backup. If it makes sense for neither of those uses, stash it in that lockbox or safe-deposit box and forget about it.

Third Step

Start exterminating your debt. My advice will contradict much of what you read in the media, where financial pros suggest you start the process with the card carrying the most onerous interest rate. That strategy doesn't take into account the psychology of money. Instead, I advocate that you begin with the card carrying the lowest balance. Success in all areas of money management stems in part from a positive-feedback loop. You see positive results, so you feel good about your efforts, and feeling good about your efforts leads to a continuation of those efforts, which, in turn, continues to produce positive results. Outside of winning the lottery and miraculously having the wealth to repay all your debts at once, this positive feedback is absolutely essential to successfully erasing your consumer debt.

Despite advice you might read in the financial media, consolidating all your balances on a single card, even if that card charges a low rate, isn't the best route. You are subverting the psychology of money. Again, if you see a huge balance on your statement every month, and you don't see that your monthly payments are eating into that balance to any real degree, you will feel discouraged and lose whatever impetus to eradicate your debts you originally felt. I'd rather see you continue to pay a bit more in interest, but experience the success of systematically paying off each credit card.

The Worst Idea You Can Have

Commonly, people who find themselves saddled with big credit-card balances think: "I might as well buy what I want, because it's not like this one additional purchase will put me that much more in the hole." Bad, bad idea. Such a situation might unfold something like this: You have, let's say, $10,000 in debt, an amount that causes you financial stress. You're paying it off, but the progress is slow and frustrating. Come Friday night, you and your spouse want to go to dinner and you two are choosing between a low-cost family-style buffet that might set you back $20 combined, and a high-end steak house that will ring up a bill of $150. You're tired, you're frustrated, you want to feel affluent for a while, you want to treat yourself. And the rationale you use is, "Might as well have the steaks, because it's not like another $150 is going to mean that much on our credit card."

Such thinking undermines the get-out-of-debt mentality necessary to successful debt-reduction management. Not only are you adding more helium to your debt balloon, you are effectively telling yourself you're a failure. Soon enough you slowly abandon your debt-repayment scheme entirely, leading to further feelings of failure and to the feeling that you are hopelessly in hock and, therefore, might as well spend to feel better about life. This is the negative-feedback loop that spirals inexorably toward bankruptcy and financial ruin.

It's a Lifestyle

To keep moving in a productive direction means you need to see and feel the positive effects of progress. So make a list of all your credit cards, and next to each write the currently outstanding balance. Start reducing the debt on the smallest balance and pay it off as quickly as possible. Once you zero the balance on that card, move to the next-lowest balance and begin the process all over again. The momentum of having achieved your goal on one card will naturally motivate you to zero the balance on that next card.

Make no mistake, though. This won't be as easy as those last few paragraphs might suggest. Eliminating onerous debt is a lifestyle issue, and your lifestyle will necessarily be affected. You cannot expect to pay off your consumer debt if you continue your consumer ways. You cannot spend your discretionary dollars as you currently do. That will accomplish nothing.

Instead, you must redirect at least 75 percent of those discretionary dollars into debt repayment. The remaining 25 percent you should spend on the items that bring you and your family a sense of joy or happiness. Again, this is a psychology of money issue. If you feel debt reduction is preventing you from enjoying every aspect of your life, you will forsake your plan and continue foundering in a pool of debt.

With that 75 percent of your discretionary income, you will split your debt repayment into three slices. The first slice repays all the debt you accumulate in the current month on your primary card—and, remember, you should be accumulating very little, since you are not in consumer mode. The second slice goes to paying the minimum balance due on each of the cards you've put away.

That third slice, whatever is left, is the most important. It goes entirely to paying down the smallest balance. If that third slice of money isn't enough to cover even the minimum due on the card with the smallest balance, then either you are still spending too much on consumer purchases during the month on your primary card, or your debt is simply too large for your income to handle. If you're spending too much, this inability to meet the minimum payment on all your cards is the clear proof you need that your discretionary spending must be cut to the bone and, perhaps, your fixed costs must be restructured to free additional money. Otherwise, debt will control your life.

If your debts are too large for your income to handle, you likely need the assistance of a not-for-profit credit-counseling agency. These counselors will help you work with creditors to reorganize your debts so that they're more affordable on your current income. You'll find an abundance of such agencies in your area by searching "nonprofit credit counseling" on the Internet. Or start with the National Foundation for Credit Counseling (www.nfcc.org), which offers a counselor-location service.

5

What's My Score?

To the government, you are a Social Security number. To lenders and the credit industry you are a credit score, like it or not.

Credit scores are pervasive nowadays. You cannot escape them. They dictate whether a consumer-credit company will lend you money and, if so, at what rate. They play a starring role in mortgage applications and can determine whether a landlord will rent to you or whether the local utility company will require that you pony up a deposit for an electrical hookup.

The three-digit number that is your score is a snapshot of your history as a borrower, encapsulating years' worth of prompt payments or a lackadaisical attitude toward repaying lenders. The higher your score, the greater the probability a lender will deem you creditworthy and the lower your cost of borrowing. The inverse is also true: The lower your score, the more reluctant lenders are to front you the money, and that will manifest itself in higher interest rates, which obviously increases your cost of borrowing.

Along with your credit score, lenders also scrutinize your credit report. These are two different though interrelated products. Where your credit score is the equivalent of a movie trailer that reveals the essence of your financial story line, your credit report is the film itself—more like a documentary—chronicling the ups and downs and plot twists that have occurred during your financial life.

Though largely overlooked by the bulk of households, these numbers have a direct, immediate, and meaningful effect on your personal finances, though it all happens behind the scenes, in the fine print that no one pays attention to. Lenders make all their decisions based on what these two reports reveal. In the most practical sense, your credit score and report reach directly into your wallet, affecting how much money you pay in interest when you borrow to buy everything from a house to a car to a new television.

Consumers with the highest credit scores and a spotless credit report will pay the lowest interest rate because, in aggregate, they represent the lowest risk to lenders, based on historical repayment patterns. Consumers with the lowest credit scores and a sketchy credit report will pay the highest interest rates because they represent a far greater risk of default, meaning the lender faces a great probability that it might not get back the money it has loaned to the buyer to make the purchase. On relatively inexpensive items, such as a $1,000 TV, the ultimate cost might be less than $100 over the course of a three-year repayment cycle. Yet on substantially larger purchases, such as the cost of repaying a $250,000 mortgage over thirty years, the difference in having a high credit score and a low score can be $50,000 to $100,000 or more in additional interest payments, depending on prevailing interest rates—in other words, real money.

Examine Your Report and Learn Your Score

Chances are pretty good you don't know your credit score at the moment and probably haven't seen your credit report in eons, if ever. The agencies that gather the data that determine both do not routinely alert you to either your score or your report unless you've signed up for one of the various credit-monitoring services they sell. Instead, you'll need to go in search of the information yourself.

All three major credit-reporting agencies—Experian (www .experian.com), TransUnion (www.transunion.com), and Equifax (www.equifax.com)—will sell to you copies of your credit report whenever you want it. However, you have a cheaper option. By law you can obtain for free a copy of your credit report from each provider once a year through AnnualCreditReport.com. Doing so is wise. Examining your report at least annually will reveal any potential problems you might need to address.

Identity theft, for instance, is a substantial and growing problem, and examining your credit report will show you if any unauthorized credit cards exist that are tied to your Social Security number. In similar fashion, a credit report will spotlight any potential flaws that might be affecting your credit score, since scores are based on your credit report. Creditors are not always 100 percent accurate in the information they report to the credit-reporting agencies, and the agencies, too, make their own mistakes. Knowing the error exists is the only way to correct it, and the only way to know it exists is to see the error appear on your credit report.

Understanding Your Score

Unlike credit reports, credit scores are not available for free annually. If you want to know your score, you have to pay to obtain it from any of the three credit-rating agencies, which will charge between five and ten dollars. Though the agencies operate independently, they provide credit scores as part of a joint venture that filters your credit history through a uniform scoring model and produces a number called the VantageScore. Assuming your three credit reports look fine to you, then obtaining your credit score—your VantageScore—from just a single provider is enough to show you how lenders see your creditworthiness.

VantageScores range from 501 to 990, and are divided into quintiles that produce letter-grade rankings similar to what you experienced in school. Based on your score, you fall into the A, B,

C, D, or F category. Good and not so good are pretty self-evident on this academic scale. The scale's range:

- 901–990 = A
- 801–900 = B
- 701–800 = C
- 601–700 = D
- 501–600 = F

Don't waste your time trying to figure out how the agencies calculate the VantageScore. The calculus is proprietary, and the characteristics that lead to higher and lower credit scores can seem counterintuitive. For instance, your credit-card company might increase your line of credit, meaning in effect that you can potentially cause even more damage to your finances. But instead of marring your score, that action actually improves your credit, assuming you don't rush out and ring up additional purchases to max out the new credit line.

To the ratings agencies, the expanded credit improves your ratio of credit used to credit available. In a simple example, the event flows through your credit score like this: You currently have a credit line of $10,000 on your card, and you're carrying a balance of $8,000, thus you've consumed 80 percent of your available credit. But then your credit-card company sends you a letter noting that, because you're such a valuable customer and have demonstrated the ability to pay your monthly bill on time, it has increased your credit line to $15,000.

Without any effort on your part, without having paid off a penny of your outstanding balance, you're now consuming only about 53 percent of your available credit. That lower credit usage will be reflected positively in your credit score because, in the most basic view, it implies that you employ credit relatively prudently.

At the end of the day, managing your credit report and keeping track of your credit score are important facets of personal finance. Though they don't put money in your pocket the way a paycheck or, maybe, a dividend payment in your brokerage account does, their ramifications for your finances are nonetheless equally meaningful, because they can cause you to pay more in interest than you otherwise might. Maintain the highest credit score and you can be assured that you're not overpaying for the capital you borrow to live your life.

Ignore your credit report and your credit score at your own risk.

Padding Your Score

Improving your credit score is a bit like steering an ocean liner—you need time and patience to turn it around.

Though Americans are clearly accustomed to immediate gratification, you won't find any quick fixes for improving your credit. It takes time to build a credit history and a credit score, and it takes time to repair one that you've destroyed, though it certainly can be done.

The rules for repair are simple:

- Pay your bills on time. This is, perhaps, the single most important rule of the bunch. Lenders want to see proof on your credit report that you will repay their money in a timely fashion.
- If you're not current on even a single credit card, get current and stay current.
- Do not spend up to the maximum limit on your card. A lower ratio of debt usage to debt available, as noted a few pages back, improves your score. If you're at the max, make an effort to meaningfully reduce your debt by following the debt-eradication plan spelled out in Chapter 4.
- Don't close accounts tied to an unused card if that card establishes a long credit history for you.

(Continued)

- Don't open new credit-card and charge-card accounts, even if you get a 10 percent savings on your initial purchases. Continually adding new accounts hurts your score.

That's it. Follow those rules and your credit scores will improve over time.

6

What Is My Road Map to Wealth?

Imagine how nice it would be to win the lottery. Maybe throw a Powerball number in the mix, too, and really pump up the millions you receive. You could pay off all your debt. Buy your kids a house. New cars for you. Wonderful travel. A secure retirement.

For many Americans, this is a financial plan. Not a good one, mind you, but a plan nonetheless. To friends and family, they'll joke about winning the lottery and finding themselves suddenly on Easy Street. But in private moments, winning the lottery isn't just their dream; it's their prayer every night, because they're convinced a lottery jackpot is their only road to wealth. That helps explain why state lotteries have expanded across the country with such zeal and why so many people effectively throw away money every week on the near-zero-percent chance that they'll win the lottery and never have to work again.

Nice dream. Alas, the road to wealth does not go through any state's lottery commission. The only wealth lotteries create is for the states themselves, since a lottery is effectively a tax on people who don't understand mathematical odds. Same goes for casinos and horse-racing tracks and sports books. These places exist because there's profit to be made, which means the bulk of the people who pony up money to bet on, well, the ponies or the craps table or a Super Bowl or a lottery draw will be financial losers. If the bulk of them were winners, the casinos and racetracks and lotteries would fail as a business in relatively short order, because they wouldn't have the money to pay off all those winning gambles.

The Real Road to Wealth

The road that will help you build real financial security for yourself and your family runs through your wallet. Just to complete my comments on the money wasted on lotteries, if you normally spend twenty dollars a week playing the lottery—and many people spend much more—and you instead funnel that cash every week into a basic savings account paying an interest rate of just 4 percent annually (remember the law of compounding?), you would amass slightly more than $60,000 over thirty years. That's real money, absolutely assured "winnings." Over the same period, you will have tossed away $31,200 on lottery tickets. Sure, thirty years seems like a long time horizon, but lottery players stop at the nearby minimart every week for decades, naively confident that their favorite set of numbers will hit this week, always returning the next week when they're wrong yet again.

I started you on the road to wealth by explaining why controlling your budget and your consumer debt are the two most important factors for attaining your definition of "rich." The next step in the process is learning to use your income to build wealth through savings and investing.

Savings Is the Cornerstone of Wealth Building

A savings account is your first line of defense in turbulent times, and a source of capital for down payments on a house or a car, and for investing in opportunities that arise in both good times and bad.

Investing, meanwhile, is the growth serum of wealth building. An investment account, either at a brokerage house or through your employer's 401(k) retirement-savings plan or through an Individual Retirement Account, is where a portion of your savings has a chance to grow into a sum much larger over time.

Net Worth

Savings and investing work together to create your overall net worth, effectively your financial barometer tracking your progress toward whatever monetary goal you set.

Net worth: Total assets (including house, cars, cash, and investments) minus total liabilities (including mortgage, home-equity loans, students loans, car loans and leases, and credit-card debt). Positive is good. Negative is bad.

Some of what you're about to read is basic personal finance, such as the need to open and routinely fund an ordinary savings account—the blocking and tackling that's fundamental to wealth building. Some of it is much more sophisticated, such as the need to spread your investments globally and to protect your overall portfolio with investments in gold, commodities, and even currencies. None of this is get-rich-quick hokum. Rich does not come quick. Poor can, though, particularly if you don't save and invest prudently and, instead, regularly pursue the next hot stock tip or money-making venture.

Once you've begun to build wealth through savings and investing, you have to protect that wealth from unforeseen events through various legal arrangements, including wills and estates and insurance. I will address these subjects in later chapters.

Let's start with the basic savings account.

Laying the Foundation: Opening a Savings Account

If you hope to be an effective steward of your money, and to pro-actively prepare your family's finances for the dark days that can arise unexpectedly, then you need to fund a savings account. In a world where your home is your castle, a savings account is your moat to keep bad things at bay.

Like the Internet connection you pay for every month, like the groceries you need to feed the family and the electricity required to power your home, savings is a bill requirement payment every month. You cannot look upon savings as an account you fund from time to time, only when you have a little extra cash, because the reality is that you will always find a way to spend that extra money and you will perennially put off building your savings.

Savings serves two purposes: First, it's that moat—the buffer between you and potential financial hardship or ruin. If you lose your job or some other financial calamity strikes, your savings account steps up to offer the monetary support you and your family need until you find new employment or the current challenges pass. Second, it's the backbone of the support you will require later in life, when your career is over, and you are living off the resources you amassed during your working days. Don't be lulled into a false sense of confidence because Social Security exists.

. Social Security won't replace all your income. The program was never designed to fund retirement, just to supplement it. Its aim is to provide in retirement only about 40 percent of your working paycheck. Chances are high that in retirement you cannot live on 40 percent of today's income, especially given the rising costs of medicine and healthcare that you will inevitably face when you're older. Also, Social Security may not exist one day. It is financially addled and in need of drastic overhaul before it's bankrupt.

Financial planners universally agree retirees will need to replace between 70 percent and 80 percent of their working income, while retirees routinely disclose in surveys that their life in retirement costs more than they originally expected, many saying they spend as much as, if not more than, they did before retirement.

Your nest egg must supply the rest. And that starts with savings.

Legendary investor Baron Rothschild once said that compound interest is the "eighth wonder of the world." Compound interest is money made by money, which continues to grow as interest is added to the principal. I once read that if the thirty pieces of silver given Judas Iscariot to betray Jesus Christ had been invested tax free at just 4 percent compounded, after 2,000 years the resulting total would have provided $300,000 for each of earth's then 5 billion inhabitants. (I haven't done the math to verify this assertion, but you are welcome to test the theory.) I can't guarantee Judas's bounty, but I can give you a fundamental rule. Money at compound interest doubles in the number of years indicated by 72 divided by the interest rate. For example, if your savings account earns 4 percent interest compounded, your money will double in eighteen years. If you can obtain 8 percent compounded, the money doubles in nine years.

People often complain that they can't find the money to save and, thus, they don't. Truth is, saving is easy and relatively painless once you work it into your budget. While saving should be viewed as a fixed cost, in practical terms it actually comes out of your discretionary dollars, because it is not the same sort of contractual expense as a car payment or the monthly house note or the electric bill. So when you design your budget, the first amount deducted from your discretionary spending should be earmarked for your savings account.

Savings is, perhaps, the most important account you will own. This will tide you over the financial emergencies of life without forcing you to make rash decisions at a bad moment. The housing-inspired economic crash of 2007 and 2008 is a fine example. As the crisis gained momentum late in the summer of 2008, some major American and European banks began to fail. Housing prices had collapsed by then but were still falling monthly by record amounts. Credit had dried up, meaning businesses and consumers had trouble funding everything from payroll to a new car. Stock prices fell off a cliff. All that combined to make households retrench and to leave people feeling vulnerable financially.

In such a period, your savings allows for a sense of perspective, some calm amid the storm. Your savings buffer means you have no immediate need to adjust your life by liquidating other assets that have likely fallen in value temporarily. You might even have the flexibility to wade into the carnage and grab assets on the cheap, fortifying your finances for the long run. You don't feel pressured to react while so many around you are panicky. You will have a sense of clarity because your mind isn't racing to determine how to deal with the situation before your finances fall apart.

Even if your job is displaced by such economic upheaval, you have the luxury of time, feeling no need to accept the first job you can find, which may not be the right job for you or your family's real needs.

And if nothing else, if no financial emergency ever clouds your days, a savings account offers the peace of mind that comes simply from knowing that your family is covered just in case. That, more than anything a credit card can buy, is truly priceless.

Digging this moat—accumulating the savings—can be quite painless when you structure your finances to handle the obligation. Once you determine how much savings your budget can tolerate each month, ask your employer or your bank to redirect into your savings account that much money from your paycheck or checking account. Many companies have ties to a local credit union and through payroll deduction will automatically funnel to the credit union whatever amount you request. If that's not an option where you work, just about every bank in the nation offers a program in which you can automatically direct a particular sum of money into a savings account from your checking account on a regular basis—weekly, semiweekly, or monthly.

Either way, when money is automatically pulled from your paycheck or checking account before you get hold of it, you will naturally adjust to the new income level and won't live your life in any fundamentally different way, though you will be growing wealthier and more secure in the process.

How Much You Need in Your Savings Account

This is entirely specific to your life. Some financial professionals say three months of living expenses are adequate. Some insist on six months. Others say a year is best. The real answer for you depends on your career. If you work in a career with limited opportunities to move around from one employer to another, or in a career subject to layoffs, I encourage you to err on the side of conservatism and set aside a sum that covers as many months as you can possibly muster. Your hunt for new employment, should you ever lose your job, could take many months and might require you pay the cost of retraining yourself with more marketable skills. If, however, you work in an industry with many opportunities for employment, or you're in government or a tenured position, you can probably get by with a smaller account.

Ultimately, in a financial emergency you want your savings to cover all your mandatory costs of living. These include not just fixed costs, but a modicum of discretionary costs, such as cable TV, a restaurant meal or a movie on occasion with the family, and the Internet, which can help in your hunt for new employment. Ask yourself what number feels right. After all, money isn't just the dollars and cents on a bank statement. It's that feeling of security. If you calculate your mandatory monthly costs at $3,500, does three months of those costs—or $10,500—feel comfortable to you? If yes, fine. If no, keep adding to the balance and stop when you hit a number that strikes you as right. That's your target.

You won't reach your target immediately. Your efforts will likely require many months, maybe a few years, before you reach the number. Don't get discouraged. Just start saving monthly, and don't stop. You'll receive your bank statement in the mail one day and see that you have reached your goal.

How much you should save from each paycheck to fund your savings depends on how much you can currently afford. A widely used rule of thumb holds that you should save 10 percent of every paycheck, though more is clearly better. I know not everyone can stretch their income that far, so start with an amount that just begins to cause you a little financial distress. In other words, if saving 3 percent of your paycheck means you have to cut out a few restaurant meals and axe one of the weekly trips to the movies with the family, then 3 percent is a good beginning point. From there, your goal is to increase the percentage you save by 1 percent a year until you reach 10 percent. If, through better budgeting or after paying off certain debts, you're able to boost your savings rate by more than 1 percent a year, or you're able to save more than 10 percent of each paycheck, all the better. Your life will be well served by doing so.

To reach your ultimate goal more quickly, allocate to your savings at least half of every unexpected dollar you receive. That means every bonus you earn at work, gifts of cash, refunds, whatever nonpaycheck income you receive. This way, the unexpected income works to bulk up your savings painlessly while at the same time providing you a little extra money for enjoying your life.

Once you reach your goal, don't stop saving. Instead, redirect into other productive investments the money that you would otherwise shovel into a savings account. Pay down your mortgage, for example, or any other debts you have. Increase the sum going into your retirement savings or other investment accounts. Donate more to the charities and churches you support. Prefund a larger portion of children's college costs. You have an untold number of ways to put your money to work. Increasing your consumer spending solely because you have extra money and you don't know what to do with it isn't one of them.

Where to Save

Several options exist for where you open your savings account.

A local bank, thrift, or credit union, particularly the one where you currently have your checking account, is the obvious choice. Consider as well the various Internet banks; they're just as safe and carry the same FDIC protections that cover your hometown banks. Whatever path you choose, shop around. Money works best when it works hardest for you, and banks compete on the interest rates they offer in order to attract your deposits. All else being equal, the bank that pays you the highest interest rate is generally the better option.

Internet-based banks usually pay the highest rates because they don't have the same cost structure as do brick-and-mortar banks. Where local banks were offering 1 percent or less on basic savings in late 2008, online banks were paying 3 percent to 3.25 percent, making them a smarter choice for building the foundation of your personal finances.

Defining "Emergency"

An "unexpected" car insurance bill is not an emergency expense. Unfortunately, far too many people see it that way. The bill arrives and they have no clue how they're going to pay it. So

(Continued)

they raid their savings account or put the bill on a credit card. Either approach is bad, because you're undermining the wealth you're trying to build or putting yourself into debt—or, potentially, both.

The worst part is that this bill wasn't unexpected. You were simply unprepared. And your worry about how to cover the cost is the direct result.

Recurring yet irregular payments of all sorts must be treated as monthly bills. You know they will arise at various points throughout the year, so work them into your budget just as you do the utility bill.

Here's the catch, though: You need to separate these funds from your daily checking account, otherwise you risk spending on other purchases the money you need for the irregular expense when it arrives. The trick: Open a separate account that you draw on specifically for these irregular payments. Every month, deposit into this account an amount that over the course of a year will cover all the irregular payments you know will arise. This way, you will be prepared for those bills and won't struggle with how to pay them.

Costs to plan for include those paid quarterly, semiannually, or annually. These can include insurance premiums for life, auto, health, and long-term-care policies, or homeowner's insurance if your lender doesn't include the premium in your monthly mortgage payment; private-school tuition for your kids or various educational fees; real estate and other property taxes not included in your mortgage payment, or vehicle registration fees.

Don't limit your unexpected-payment fund to fixed expenses alone. Routine, irregular discretionary expenses arise all the time, too. The annual family vacation is, perhaps, the most obvious example. If you know you spend $3,000 a year for a week at the beach or on the ski slopes, stuffing $250 a month into your irregular-expenses fund means the money is there when the cost arises and it won't disturb your budget for the month or require that you dip into savings. Other such expenses might include the season tickets and parking pass you buy every year to attend the home games of your favorite college or professional sports team, new consumer electronics you expect to buy to replace an aging TV or computer, even the new car you'll have to buy one day to replace your current car.

Basically, any future cost you can see coming your way at some point is a cost that you can plan for by sticking an appropriate amount of money into this irregular-expense account on a regular basis.

What defines a *real* emergency? Events that would alter your family's lifestyle—the loss of a job, a fire, a natural disaster, a dire medical illness, the death of a breadwinner. These change your financial picture. Improperly budgeting for next year's auto-insurance premium should not.

Savings Beyond the Savings Account

The basic savings account isn't the only bank-based option you have for savings. Also useful are money-market accounts and certificates of deposit.

Money-market accounts, sometimes identified as MMAs or even "high-yield savings accounts," typically offer slightly higher rates than do savings accounts. Banks can afford to pay higher rates because they put your money to work in what is literally the "money market," a marketplace where banks and other institutions borrow from one another for terms of one year or less.

At banks, money-market accounts are FDIC insured. At credit unions, the National Credit Union Administration (a federal agency) protects your cash on deposit. The point: In a money market, your dollars are government guaranteed if anything ever happens to the financial institution you select.

Unlike savings accounts, however, money-market accounts generally require a minimum balance, often in the $500 to $2,500 range. Allow the account to slip below that level and you will be hit with a monthly fee and the possibility that you lose interest accrual during the time your balance is below the minimum. Moreover, money markets typically limit the number of transactions you can conduct in a month, though usually on the withdrawal side only. You can deposit as much money as you wish and on as many occasions as necessary, but federal law limits monthly withdrawals to no more than six transfers to other accounts or three payments outside the bank.

What's in a Name?

Don't assume that a "money-market" fund is a "money-market account."

While banks offer money-market *accounts*, brokerage firms offer money-market *funds*. The two are not interchangeable, though you will often find them wrongly conflated on some financial do-it-yourself websites.

Money-market funds, often called "money funds," are mutual funds, not savings accounts. They aim to maintain a constant one-dollar net asset value, or NAV, the price of the fund. Instead of paying interest, as do bank money-market accounts, funds generate a rate of return that is paid to the account in terms of additional, fractional shares. Money funds are also more liquid, meaning you can access the cash at any time, without any penalty and without any withdrawal limitations.

Though savers often assume a money-market fund is as safe as a money-market account, that's not necessarily true. Yes, they are safe, relatively speaking. But while money funds are widely considered low-risk, because the NAV is not guaranteed you can lose money.

Indeed, during the mortgage-inspired financial meltdown in late summer 2008, the Primary Fund, one of the original money funds, "broke the buck," the industry euphemism that colorfully describes what happens when the NAV sinks below one dollar. As the crisis gained momentum, the Primary Fund's shares closed at one point at ninety-seven cents, a 3 percent loss. That's not terribly large, of course, but when you're investing for rock-solid safety any loss is just short of horrific.

Moreover, money funds carry no FDIC protection. So if you happen to be in a fund that breaks the buck, the FDIC doesn't have to make your account whole.

Certificates of deposit, or CDs, generally earn even higher rates than money-market accounts, depending upon how long you're willing to part with your money. The longer you agree to leave your money untouched, the larger the interest rate a bank is usually willing to pay. (On occasion, economic periods will arise in which longer-term interest rates are at or below short-term rates, what market pundits know as an "inverted yield curve." In those moments, longer-term CDs will pay interest rates that are equal to and often less than shorter-term CDs.)

Interest rates on CDs can be markedly higher than those on savings and money-market accounts because of the amount of time you're willing to let the bank put your money to work. Where a $10,000 money-market account was paying about 2.75 percent on average nationally in late 2008, a one-year CD was paying about 4 percent on average. Five-year CDs were paying more than 4.6 percent. With large balances, banks often sweeten the interest rate. At $100,000, what banks call a "jumbo CD," rates for a one-year deposit were as high as 4.65 percent at some banks in late 2008. Five-year jumbos offered as much as 5.25 percent.

CDs are a fine place to stash cash, such as your emergency savings, that you do not expect to need for some period of time.

The higher interest rate means your money is working harder for you.

Like money-market accounts, CDs typically mandate a minimum investment to open the account, often $500 to $1,000. They are government insured, as well, in case of problems with your bank at some point.

The risk with a CD is that your money is supposedly locked away. You can withdraw it in an emergency, if necessary, but you will pay a price, usually forsaking three months of interest payments.

Laddering, the art of combining liquidity with income, is one of the savvier strategies with CDs. It's a simple process of stretching over multiple maturity dates all the money you want to invest in CDs. In a basic example, you might put one-fifth of your money into five different CDs with annual maturity dates ranging between one and five years. The benefit here is twofold: you have access to some portion of your money every year, yet the bulk of it remains invested for the longer haul, earning greater returns. Each year, as a CD matures, if you don't need the cash you just roll it over into another five-year CD (remember, all your other CDs will have one year less time remaining, so your original five-year investment is now down to four years, meaning you need another five-year CD to top off the ladder).

Laddering is a particularly useful strategy for times when interest-rate movements are uncertain. In those periods, guessing what rates might do exposes you to the risk of being wrong. You might keep all your money in short-term CDs expecting rates will soon rise, thereby allowing you to lock in a higher rate at some point. But if rates fall instead, you've lost that gamble, because when it's time to roll over your current CD, you will earn a lower rate than previously. With a ladder, you will still earn that lower rate on the money rolled over, but you'll also have those longer-term CDs locked in at higher rates for a while.

At times when rates are rising, you want to be in shorter-term CDs so that your maturity dates arrive fairly frequently, offering you the chance to roll into a higher rate. Conversely, in periods of falling interest rates, you generally want your money in longer-dated CDs that lock you into the highest possible rates, leaving your money unaffected even as interest rates slip.

7

What Is My Engine to Wealth?

Investing is the next step in wealth building after you've established your savings account. The aim of investing, at its core, is simple: to earn profits by putting your capital at risk.

In a savings account you're taking no risk. The money you deposit is guaranteed by the government; it will always be there when you need it. The money you invest outside of savings is money you specifically want to put at risk in the hope of earning returns dramatically greater than you'll ever earn on your savings. It may not be there when you need it, or the value of your original capital might be sharply reduced. With investing, the only guarantee is that there are no guarantees.

But no guarantee is no reason to avoid investing and, instead, stash all your money in savings and CDs. If nothing else, investing serves one very useful purpose: It helps your nest egg outpace the ravages of inflation.

> **Inflation:** The tendency of prices to rise over time. Inflation is measured broadly by the federal government's monthly Consumer Price Index, the CPI. Historically, inflation increased at an annualized rate of 3.3 percent between 1913, when U.S. Department of Labor statistics began, and late summer 2008.

Every year, for the most part, living your life grows increasingly more expensive. Interest rates on savings accounts, CDs, money-market accounts, and U.S. Treasury bonds—the safe investments—do not keep pace with inflation. Thus, your dollars in those accounts are actually losing value. That's often a hard concept for people to grasp. After all, if you have $10,000 in a savings account this year, and next year you have $10,400 thanks to a 4 percent yield, you'd seem to be ahead of the game because you have more money today than you did yesterday.

But what if inflation was running at an annualized rate of 5.8 percent, as it was in the summer of 2008? The same amount of goods you could buy with your original $10,000 on the day you deposited the money would cost a year later $10,580. Your money actually lost $180 worth of purchasing power. You don't see a physical loss of cash in your savings account, but your savings account has grown weaker in the course of a single year. Its ability to pay for your life has diminished.

Now, apply that across decades. You end up with a dollar that has no hope of paying your costs later in life unless you make it work harder than is possible in a savings account. That's where investing takes over, and that's why understanding the risks and rewards that define the various investment options is so crucial. Many people seek to avoid investments precisely because of the risk. But risk can be mitigated. And if you don't take on some risk, then, as the inflation example above showed you, your standard of living is certain to fall victim to inflation over time.

Investing

Perhaps nothing defines the U.S. economy more than the corner of Wall and Broad streets in Lower Manhattan, a compact cityscape of neoclassical facades. There on the southwest corner sits the

New York Stock Exchange, from which breathes the essence of the American brand of capitalism.

Roughly half of all Americans participate in the stock market in some fashion, either directly through a brokerage account, or indirectly through mutual funds purchased in a 401(k) retirement-savings plan, an Individual Retirement Account, a 529 College Savings Plan, or in other ways. The stock market, broadly defined to include mutual funds that own stocks, is the primary form of investment for most Americans. I'm not including a personal residence, because your home, while ostensibly an "investment," is first and foremost a shelter for your family.

But investing goes well beyond Wall Street. Along with stocks, there are all manner of corporate, municipal, and government bonds that help fund operations from Washington, D.C., to Walla Walla, Washington; mutual funds from plain vanilla index funds and single-country funds to highly volatile funds that go up when some market goes down; real estate, from direct ownership of a rental home to investment trusts that own dozens of hospitals, shopping malls, and office towers around the world; gold and commodities such as wheat, oil, and pork bellies used for making bacon; currencies, from the U.S. dollar to the euro, the yen, and the Swiss franc that you can trade against one another or that you can own directly through savings accounts and CDs; and options and futures contracts that let you gamble on the direction of price movements or that provide opportunities to hedge your portfolio against market weakness. The list is quite long.

Stocks

The stock market is not a surgery suite. By that I mean that investing in stocks is not as difficult as people generally want to assume it is. If you can draw with a crayon a picture of what Wal-Mart does, you can pretty much succeed as an investor on Wall Street.

A stock is simply a piece of paper connoting your partial ownership of some company. Own a single share of Wal-Mart and you own the right to claim a portion of the earnings Wal-Mart generates every year. You get to claim a portion of the money Wal-Mart distributes to its shareholders every year in the form of a dividend. You get to vote on issues that Wal-Mart puts to it shareholders annually. And you get to participate in Wal-Mart's growth as it opens more stores, attracts more shoppers, and earns more money through the years, thereby making each share of Wal-Mart stock more valuable over time.

That's its. That's a stock. That's as difficult as it gets.

Companies will sometimes have two types of stock—common stock and preferred stock. Common stock holders represent the lowest link on the food chain. These are the investors at greatest risk of loss if a company sinks, but who also have the greatest possibility for gain if a company's fortunes soar. At its most basic level, common stock represents equity ownership in a company and provides voting rights to each shareholder. Common stock entitles the holder to a share of the company's success through capital appreciation (the rising value of the shares in the stock market) and through dividends, which are a piece of the company's profit stream. On the downside, common stockholders are the last to be paid if a company is ever liquidated. Holders of the company's bonds and other debt are repaid first, and whatever is remaining—and often nothing remains—goes proportionally to the common stockholders.

Preferred stock is higher on the food chain and acts almost like a hybrid of common shares and corporate debt. Preferred shares earn dividends just like common shares, but at a set rate that doesn't change. The share price does fluctuate, but not nearly to the degree the common shares can, often floating in a fairly narrow range just a few dollars above or below the par value, the price at which the shares were initially issued. Preferred stock doesn't benefit from a company's expansion to the same degree common shares can.

Like debt holders, preferred shares have no voting rights. However, preferred shareholders always receive their dividend before common shareholders do, and in the event a company falls into bankruptcy, preferred shareholders have a greater claim on assets than common shareholders. Some corporations issue convertible preferred, which enables the holder to receive preferential dividends with an option to convert their shares into common stock in the event the common is rising.

Any type of stock represents a potential risk. Wal-Mart's stock could fall in value because the economy suffers or because Wal-Mart mismanages its business or consumers decide they no longer like shopping at Wal-Mart. You risk losing every penny you invested if Wal-Mart ceases to operate and the stock becomes worthless. You risk losing some income if Wal-Mart's profits suffer and the company halts or reduces its dividend payments.

Then again, you face the potential reward of turning a small sum of money into a significantly larger sum. Indeed, had you bought Wal-Mart stock when the company first issued shares in July 1971, the price of those shares would have grown to more than fifty-five dollars each as of mid-October 2008 from the equivalent price of just two cents a share. (For the record, Wal-Mart's stock never traded at two cents. That's what Wall Street calls a "split-adjusted price," meaning the original number of shares have been split through the years, which fast-growing companies do on occasion when their stock price has risen so high that they want to reduce the nominal price to make the shares more appealing to investors. As the shares are split, the price is reduced proportionately, so that if a $100 stock splits two for one, you end up with two shares of a $50 stock. In Wal-Mart's case, each original share has become 1,024 shares.)

Winning on Wall Street

Adhere to a few basic rules:

- **Don't constantly chase the next hot stock** chatted up by friends and family, read about on investor blogs and chat-rooms online, or promoted by mouthpieces spewing their opinion of the moment on business-news TV channels. Chances are great you will invest in a series of losers.

- **Don't look at a stock as if it's a lottery ticket.** You are buying a business, not a chance at winning millions. No business turns a few dollars into a fortune overnight. If you expect that, you're not investing, you're gambling.

- **Don't constantly trade** just because your stocks aren't moving when others are. This is expensive because of the commissions you pay and the opportunities you will inevitably miss when the stocks you were bored with suddenly start to move higher after you sell out. Different businesses and different industries move in different cycles. This is where diversification comes in, and I'll take about that in later chapters.

- **Do invest based on fundamentals.** Wal-Mart has soared in value through the years because it has proven to be a fundamentally good company, in a fundamentally good corner of the economy. The proof is in Wal-Mart's long history of consistent revenue and earnings growth, two of the key metrics when picking stocks to own. More on that coming up.

Why Stock Prices Move

Broadly speaking, the stock market, and companies in particular, move up and down in value based on numerous facts, perceptions, and expectations. Leading the pack of factors is corporate news and the broader economy. When a company is doing well, when its sales and profits are growing from quarter to quarter, year to year, that tends to push the share price higher, either quickly or in fits and starts. Conversely, bad news—that is, slowing or falling sales and profit growth—has the opposite effect. This "news" could be real, the actual, reported results the company announces every quarter, or it could be based on investor expectations of what the news will ultimately show or perceptions that business is better or worse than the company's current results indicate.

Google has been a fine example of all of this. Since it became a public company in August 2004, revenue and earnings at the Internet's most popular search engine have grown at hyperbolic rates of between roughly 40 percent and more than 100 percent from 2004 to mid-2008. The news of strong growth sent Google's shares surging, as did expectations. The stock rose from its $85-per-share initial offering price, its IPO, to more than $700 at one point.

But in late 2007, perceptions changed. A data provider that tracks website traffic projected that fewer web surfers were clicking on the on screen ads that generate a portion of Google's revenue. Word spread among investors and the Wall Street analysts paid to produce the "buy, sell, hold" investment ratings on stocks. The Internet darling was done, the crowd presumed. The analysts expected that fewer clicks would mean shrinking revenues, so they lowered their earnings estimates for the company and reduced the price they thought the shares were worth. Google was merely mortal after all. The shares fell sharply.

And then reality caught up with perceptions. Google, a company that generally lets its financial results do all the talking, released its quarterly financial report in early 2008. Revenue had not tailed off. Earnings had not fallen. Perceptions had been wrong all along. The shares soared again.

This is the way Wall Street works every day. It is a constant tug of war between truth and rumors, perceptions and reality.

Adding to that mix are industry trends and the broader economy, both of which exert their own influences on stock prices for good or ill. The airline industry is a fine example. When oil prices raced toward $150 a barrel in 2008, airline stocks lost tremendous altitude. Air carriers buy millions of gallons of jet fuel annually to power their fleets, and as the price of oil rose almost unstoppably in the spring and summer of that year, airlines' costs soared. Worse, the economy was sinking toward recession, a time when corporations are stingier with travel dollars, meaning fewer business trips, while consumers reel in their spending by cutting discretionary expenses such as vacations.

The combined effect leads to lower revenues from fewer travelers and rising costs from escalating oil prices, both of which conspire to pinch the companies' profits, sending investors fleeing the industry. When oil prices are moderate or low, and the economy is strong, airline stocks generally soar because their costs are more manageable and travelers are abundant.

Stock Terms Simplified

Revenue: The amount of money flowing into a company's cash registers from whatever it sells to its customers. Out of this revenue stream come all the costs the company has to pay, such as salaries, taxes, advertising, and supplies. Revenue is also known as sales or the "top line." Investors pay attention to revenue growth because it is one of the few items on an income statement that can't be manipulated as easily as others, and it's an indication of how well the company is attracting new business.

Profits: The amount of money remaining after paying all the bills and taxes and other costs that must be deducted from the revenue stream. This is, in essence, how much money a company puts into its corporate savings account every year after paying off every cost. Profit is also known as net profits, earnings, or the proverbial "bottom line." Though profits can be manipulated—and routinely are—by a variety of accounting measures, investors home in on so-called per-share earnings (net profits divided by the number of shares outstanding), since stocks are ultimately valued based on a company's underlying earnings.

P/E ratio: Price divided by per-share earnings.

Ultimately, a stock is nothing more than the perceived value of its earnings or the long-range value of its dividend stream, assuming the company pays a dividend, since not all do.

The more valuable investors perceive those earnings to be, the higher the multiple they're willing to pay to own the shares—and vice versa. By multiple I mean the price-earnings multiple, what Wall Street insiders refer to as the P/E ratio. This is nothing more than the price of the stock (the "P") divided by the per-share earnings (the "E"). A thirty-dollar stock with three dollars per share in earnings yields a P/E ratio of 10.

P/E ratios range widely depending on company, industry, and economy, among other factors. What might seem low to one company in one industry is average to another company in another industry. Grocery stores, generally speaking, are not fast-growth companies. Technology companies generally are. Thus, a supermarket chain such as SuperValu has historically traded at a P/E multiple in the low teens. By contrast, software giant Microsoft has grown rapidly through the years and has a multiple that is basically double SuperValu's. That doesn't necessarily make Microsoft a better stock, it just means investors value Microsoft's earnings more richly because of expectations that the tech company will grow its sales and earnings at a faster pace. Over the years, Microsoft has grown its sales and earnings by amounts in the midteens to mid-20 percent range. SuperValu's sales and earnings have grown by low- to mid-single-digit rates.

But even within sectors differences emerge. Whole Foods Market competes in the same industry as SuperValu, though clearly at the high end. Whole Foods' sales and earnings growth has been much closer to that of Microsoft. The result is that investors traditionally have awarded Whole Foods a higher P/E ratio than they have its industry neighbor SuperValu.

Perception Rules Prices

The problem, as you might recognize, is that when investors base stock prices on perceptions, situations arise in which a particular stock, a certain industry, or the market as a whole is either wildly exuberant or depressingly morose. Neither attitude might be accurate. That one of those moments has arrived is sometimes apparent, though often it's not, because the stock market spends much of its life moving back and forth from one side of that spectrum to the other. Sometimes the moves are driven by market fundamentals, other times stock-price movements seem as random as the toss of the dice. (I'm not going to detail how to divine the fundamentals. Many books have been written on that subject. Pick one or more of those if you want a deeper understanding of how investors value stocks and analyze a company's financial statements.)

No matter where on the spectrum you find the market, an industry, or a single stock at some particular moment, the playbook is the same: You have to determine *your* perception of the investments you own or the opportunities you're interested in pursuing. The wisest decisions are almost always made independently of the crowd. When investors are rushing in and every pundit you hear is screaming "buy, buy, buy," step back and consider whether it's time to sell based on the fundamentals. Perceptions might have moved so far ahead of reality that taking some profits off the table and awaiting a more rational environment is the smarter strategy.

And when it seems that every investor is diving for the exit, and the talking heads are bemoaning a falling sky, look for the buying opportunities. In those moments, stocks might be priced well below their fair value, letting you in on the cheap before the market as a whole recognizes it overshot the downside yet again and pushed an otherwise good company to unrealistically low levels.

The P/E ratio is a good way to determine that a stock is at unrealistically low levels, or even exuberantly priced. A company's shares will typically trade within a historical range, and that history could be anywhere from five to twenty-five years or longer. If shares are trading well below that range, the stock may be a bargain. Above the range, it may be overpriced.

I say "may" because no rule on Wall Street is set in stone. Company dynamics change, and when that happens investors recalibrate the P/E ratio accordingly, either up or down depending on the circumstances. Shares that fall below their historical range, for instance, are not always a good buy; they could be falling for good reasons, such as decaying fundamentals. For decades, General Motors was an American blue chip, a stalwart of the New York Stock Exchange, a safe investment for just about any portfolio. Yet by the late nineties and into the 2000s, you could see the collision coming. GM's fundamentals were weakening, hurt by a rash of lower-priced, higher-quality Asian imports, among other woes, and a U.S. labor force that kept the carmaker's expenses too high. By late 2004, the shares were at roughly forty dollars, less than half their value in early 2000. Had you chosen that moment to buy GM, a moment when the shares seemed a giveaway at a P/E ratio of about eight, you would have been grabbing at a falling knife—and would have lost a few fingers in the process. GM was still a fundamentally flawed company, and the stock by late 2008 had crashed to less than five dollar a share, a price GM hadn't seen since the late 1940s.

Dividends

Dividends can help value a stock and create a floor under the share price. Some Wall Street pros will rely on a mathematical model that calculates the net present value of future dividend payments to determine a stock's current worth. That's a mouthful of mathematical jargon to basically say that a stock is worth all of its future dividend payments discounted back to today. Essentially, if you know a stock will pay you $100 in dividends over the next ten years, then that stock has a particular value today.

Problem is, you don't know if that $100 will actually arrive. As the GM example shows, corporate circumstances can change dramatically in a relatively short time. GM's downfall forced the company to slash its dividend. Companies are quite proud of their dividends; some will even include in their marketing campaign the fact that they've paid a dividend for fifty years, more than a century, or whatever. Thus, they are loath to cut their dividend because of the underlying message it sends—our business is struggling. But it does happen. In October 2008, amid panic in the banking sector fueled by the ever-expanding housing crisis, Bank of America, which had paid an ever-increasing dividend for years, was forced to slash its dividend payment in half to conserve capital at a time when the banking industry and the economy were on the verge of ruin.

So, you cannot simply own a stock for its dividend stream. Even the strongest companies will cut or curtail their dividend payments on occasion. When that happens, the share price is usually whacked. In the days immediately following Bank of America's dividend cut, its stock price fell by nearly half. To be sure, that occurred during a particularly volatile moment on Wall Street, as the stock market crashed, the economy trembled, and global markets melted down. Nevertheless, a dividend cut is never good news for a stock's price.

That's largely because dividends provide a floor for the stock's price. A number of academic studies, as well as market history, have shown that in a run-of-the-mill bear market, dividend-paying stocks hold up far better than their non-dividend-paying peers. The reason: Investors often own dividend-paying stocks specifically for that consistent quarterly payment, and when stock prices fall they don't rush to dump their shares. While the stock will still weaken, at some level it generally stabilizes, even as other companies continue down, because the dividend payment—defined by the stock's dividend yield—entices investor into the shares. The stock price may not be headed higher any time soon, they concede, but at least the company is paying them a nice dividend to wait.

Amid a stock-market crash, however, all bets are off. Crashes incite panic, and panic leads to uninformed selling as investors dump stocks to raise cash out of fear that not doing so will lead to ever-deeper losses. It's at those moments that judiciously wading into the carnage can lead you to otherwise strong companies with big dividend payments that are going to survive the bloodletting.

> **Dividend yield:** Annual dividend payment divided by stock price. Yields, like P/E ratios, run the gamut from less than 1 percent to 10 percent or more, depending upon company and industry. And like P/E ratios, yields that are above or below historical norms can signal an expensive or a cheap stock. If a yield is higher than normal, the stock might be cheap; lower than normal and it might be too expensive. But beware: Exceedingly high yields can signal trouble, since they mean the stock price is deeply depressed, a sign that investors have lost faith in a company for whatever reason. These are the companies most likely to cut their dividends to conserve cash.

8

What if I Don't Like Risk?

Where a share of stock shows that you own a small part of some company, a bond implies that a company owes you some money. Bondholders are creditors, so think of yourself as the bank that has loaned money to a company.

Bonds

Corporations, as well as state, local, and federal governments both here and overseas, sell bonds. They do so to raise the cash needed to fund various projects. A company might sell bonds to help build a manufacturing facility, while your local school board might sell municipal bonds to construct new schools. The federal government sells bonds—called Treasury bonds—to finance its debt, wars, and other expenses. Companies repay bonds through the revenues generated by the business. Governments repay through the taxes they raise or, in some cases, the fees generated by some specific project the bond originally funded.

Unlike stocks, bonds don't pay a quarterly dividend. Instead, most pay a semiannual interest payment, called a coupon payment, determined by the interest rate the company established when it first sold the bonds. Nor do bonds participate as the company's sales and earnings grow. If Merck's stock price tripled at some point because the pharmaceutical giant discovered a vaccine that killed the AIDS virus or a drug that cured cancer, the company's bonds would do very little. That's because a bond represents a loan, and the only obligation a company has is to pay you the set interest payments and to return the original loan amount. Most bonds are originally sold at a $1,000 par value, the face value of the bond, and that's the amount the company repays at maturity. So while a stock could surge from $25 to $250, the bond won't rally to $2,000 or more, because the company will only return $1,000 to the bondholder.

By and large, bonds are considered a safe investment because of the promise that the company or the government will return your original principal when the bond matures. Along that road to maturity you simply collect the string of interest payments as your investment return. Maturity dates can stretch from a few months to several decades. The Walt Disney Co. famously sold 100-year bonds in 1993 that will mature in 2093—assuming the movies-and-amusement-park company is still around. For the most part, shorter-term bonds carry the smallest interest rates while longer-term bonds carry much higher rates, and for an obvious reason. The risk that a company or a government will default, that it will not be able to pay the interest payments due or return the principal, in the next three months is smaller than the risk of default 10 or 20 or 100 years from now, and investors demand higher payment to assume greater risk.

That's a bond in a nutshell.

But that's not all there is to understand about the bond market. First, not all bonds are safe. Moreover, bonds trade above and below their par value all the time. And while the interest payments are the primary concern of investors, bonds can offer capital appreciation potential just as a stock does.

Bonds and Risk

You will likely have heard the phrase "the full faith and credit of the U.S. government." Those words are generally applied to U.S. Treasury debt, and define a measure of risk. In this case, it's the assumed absence of risk, because the full faith and credit of the U.S. government implies that the American government—despite its massive and mounting debts—will stand behind its debt and will repay all interest and principal due in a timely manner. For that reason, U.S. Treasury bonds are considered the gold standard in the debt market, presenting what investors call a "risk-free rate of return," a phrase meaning that if you hold a U.S. Treasury obligation to maturity you will never lose a penny of principal or interest. Thus, you have zero risk.

At the opposite of the spectrum is junk, the name euphemistically attached to certain bonds because of the company's financial situation. These junk bonds—also called high-yield bonds—are larded with risk and represent some of the highest default rates in the bond world.

In between Treasury and junk is a wide range of bonds spanning all levels of risk. Helping investors navigate the various risks are ratings agencies such as Standard & Poor's, Moody's Investors Service, and others that regularly rate bonds based upon the underlying financial health of the specific company, national government, or local municipality. At S&P, bond ratings stretch from AAA at the very top to D at the nadir. S&P Ratings of AAA down to BBB are considered "investment-grade" bonds. BB and below are junk-bond territory, also known as non-investment-grade or high-yield bonds. Moody's ratings, and those published by other agencies, differ slightly.

These ratings help determine what interest rate a bond will carry. U.S. Treasury debt typically offers the lowest interest rates, because the risks are nearly nonexistent. You will receive your interest payments, and the Treasury Department will return your original principal at the bond's maturity. Period.

Riskier issues, meanwhile, require that companies and governments entice investors with a bigger interest rate to compensate for the risk the investor is accepting. And everything below a Treasury carries default risk to some degree. The state of Washington's

Public Power Supply System in the early 1980s canceled construction on a nuclear-power project that wildly overran its costs, and with no way to repay the debt, the power company defaulted on $2.5 billion in municipal bonds that were originally rated as investment-grade, meaning they were highly rated.

Such events are exceedingly rare with investment-grade debt, but they still happen. As I write this in late 2008, Jefferson County, Alabama, was facing the largest municipal-bond default in history—some $3.2 billion. The county found itself swamped by interest payments that had unexpectedly tripled, the result of political leaders' heeding the advice of Wall Street bankers who pitched the county on a particular bond strategy that backfired.

Junk bonds, meanwhile, are called junk for a reason. They have historically experienced a greater default rate than have investment-grade bonds, and by an exceedingly wide margin. Junk bonds generally come from companies with balance sheets that are financially weak or are already overly leveraged by other debt obligations that must be repaid. A bad patch in the economy or the loss of a significant customer can unravel a company and leave junk-bond holders with little to show for their investment except an intricately engraved bond certificate worth nothing.

That said, junk bonds can be lucrative, and can have a place in some portfolios. Because of that relationship I mentioned between risk and rates, junk bond yields are routinely much higher than you'll find on investment-grade bonds. Owning junk bonds, then, can enhance the overall returns in a portfolio. But if you're going to own junk bonds, do so in a junk-bond mutual fund, where professional bond managers are paid to sift through the complex financials and covenants specific to each bond to determine which ones are better than others to own. You don't want to go off randomly snapping up junk bonds just because of a big yield. You're taking on too much default risk. In a fund, that same bond might well default, but the loss is spread across hundreds of bonds worth hundreds of millions of dollars, so the pain is negligible. In your personal portfolio, the default of a single bond can be devastating. I'll explain more about bond funds in a moment, and mutual funds in general later.

Along with default risk, all bonds including Treasury bonds also come packaged with interest-rate risk. The purest reason to own a bond is to capture the interest payment. But if interest rates in the broader economy rise to a level that exceeds the rate paid by the bond you own, well, you'll awaken one morning to find that the bond you own is suddenly worth less than its par value. Investors, logically, want to own bonds that pay higher rates, making your bond less attractive to buyers and, thus, less valuable. The good news: If you never sell your bond, the fall in price is irrelevant, since the bond issuer will repay you the par value—assuming, of course, the company doesn't first default on those bonds.

Turns out bonds aren't always as safe as commentators sometimes make them out to be.

Bonds and Yield and, Sometimes, Capital Appreciation

As I said, about the only reason you own a bond is to capture the interest payment over some predetermined period. This payment generates what the bond community calls "yield," a calculation fairly similar to the dividend yield on a stock.

> **Bond yield:** Annual interest payment divided by a bond's current price. This is also known as "current yield."

You might think the work has already been done for you when you buy a bond. After all, if you're buying, say, a U.S. Treasury bond that matures in 2018 and has an interest rate of 4.5 percent, then there's your yield.

Ah, if only it were so simple.

The 4.5 percent is the stated rate, the initial rate the bond paid when it was first issued at its $1,000 par value. If you buy the bond directly from the government, or directly from a company if you're buying corporate bonds, then, yes, this is the yield you're going to receive—for the most part.

Once a bond starts trading in the secondary market, meaning it's changing hands among investors, its price can rise above par or fall below it. With each price change, the yield fluctuates. Here's how it works: A $1,000 bond that pays a 7 percent yield will distribute to you an annual interest check of $70. No matter where the price of that bond goes, up or down, it will always pay $70 a year until it matures. Thus, if the bond's price in the market falls to, say, $980, then the yield rises to 7.14 percent, or $70 divided by $980. Similarly, if the bond's price increases to $1,125, the yield slides to 6.22 percent. You will hear this referred to as the "inverse relationship" between yield and price—as price falls, yield rises; and as price rises, yield falls. (Just so you'll know, bond prices are quoted missing a zero. So if you see a bond priced at 97.50, the real price is $975.00. Simply move the decimal point one place to the right to see the real price in the market.)

From there, true complexity overtakes the bond market.

The *real* yield on a bond isn't the stated yield—unless you buy it precisely at par—it's the yield to maturity, the yield you will receive based upon the remaining interest payments plus the capital appreciation or depreciation you will record when the bond is redeemed. Because bonds routinely trade above or below par, you will have a profit or a loss at maturity. Profits add to the cumulative interest payments, increase the overall yield; losses subtract from total interest payments and, thus, reduce the overall yield.

And then there's yield to call, just to complicate matters further. I won't run through the details of this except to say that some bonds can be "called," meaning the company or government that issues them redeems them early, either at face value or slightly above. Callable bonds often have multiple call dates, so your ultimate yield will depend on when the bond is called and at what price, and the price you originally paid for the bonds when you bought them.

Bond issuers might call in a bond, to give just one example, if the bond was originally issued years earlier when interest rates were high and rates today are sharply lower. Calling those bonds and reissuing the debt would reduce the issuer's interest payments. Investors who buy callable bonds, particularly at a time when interest rates are falling, will pay attention to one final yield—the so-called yield to worst. This measures the yield to the first possible call date, which marks the worst possible yield outcome, because, as in investor, it limits the number of interest payments you will receive.

Bonds Versus Bond Funds

Owning a bond fund is not the same as owning a bond. The risk is entirely different, even if you concentrate your purchases in the exact same kinds of bonds.

Bond funds are an amalgamation of hundreds of bonds, and your ownership of the fund gives you proportional ownership of all those bonds and all the income and profits and losses those bonds generate. Sounds just like a bond.

And then the road diverges...

Bond funds have no maturity date, an important factor for a key reason: You can hold a single bond through thick and thin and know for certain that you will recoup your original principal at a certain date in the future, assuming no defaults, of course. Bond funds offer no such guarantee. If the bonds in the fund's portfolio fall in value or if the fund manager's bond-picking skills are terrible, the value of the fund can fall and might never recover to levels that recoup your original investment.

(Continued)

That's not to say bond funds should be avoided. They provide the easiest way for investors in 401(k) plans and investors with relatively limited assets to diversify quickly across multiple bonds. Bond funds are also the most practical means of building exposure to high-yield bonds (those junk bonds from a few pages back), as well as foreign bonds, since they will help diversify your portfolio. Owning individual junk bonds and foreign bonds exposes you to too much risk.

Individual bonds, however, can be a wiser strategy in some instances, particularly if you focus your buying on U.S. Treasury bonds or high-quality, investment-grade municipal and corporate bonds. When you know you will need access to your original principal on a specific date to meet a specific need—such as a child's college costs, a new house, or maybe even a particular expense in retirement—owning individual bonds that mature near that date makes a lot of sense. You'll earn your return up to that point and then you'll recoup your cash just at the moment you need to spend it. Best of all, you will care less about the price gyrations that will occur in the meantime because they ultimately have no impact on your money.

Taxable and Nontaxable Bonds, and the Tax-Equivalent Yield

Some bonds are more taxed than others.

Depending on what type of bond you buy—Treasury, municipal, or corporate—and depending upon where you live and where the interest payments originate, your tax obligations to the federal government and your local tax agency can differ. In short, some bonds generate taxable income, some bonds generate partially taxable income, and with some bonds none of your income is taxed.

Corporate bonds suffer the greatest tax burden. Every penny of interest income you receive is taxed by state and federal governments, and generally at whatever ordinary-income-tax rate you pay. The one exception: If you own the bonds in a Roth IRA or a Roth 401(k). Any income or profits in these accounts accumulates tax-free and you can ultimately withdraw those funds tax-free.

Income generated by U.S. Treasury bonds is taxed at ordinary income rates by the federal government, but are exempt from city, state, and local taxes. "Treasury bond," by the way, is a generic term encompassing three types of debt instruments: Treasury bills, which mature in one year or less; Treasury notes, which mature between two and ten years; and Treasury bonds, which mature beyond ten years, with the most famous being the thirty-year bond.

Municipal bonds, meanwhile, are generally tax-free, so you won't pay taxes to any state or local agency or to the federal government. I say generally because, as with so many rules, this one has exceptions. The tax-free status of muni-bonds, as they're typically called, generally only extends to the state you're in. If you live in Virginia, as I do, the bonds issued by Virginian governments are exempt on Virginia income-tax returns. If you happen to earn income from muni-bonds issued by North Carolina or New York or wherever, that income is taxable in Virginia, though it remains tax-free on federal returns. Again, a caveat: Some states do not tax the income earned on other states' bonds. Along with the District of Columbia, the munificent states include Alaska, Indiana, Nevada, South Dakota, Texas, Utah, Washington, and Wyoming. Caveat number two: Any capital gains you generate buying a muni-bond below par and selling at or above par is taxable as ordinary income.

This partial or fully tax-free status means you have yet another yield to calculate: the tax-equivalent yield.

If you think about the risk-and-rate relationship I've mentioned a couple of times, you likely recognize that corporate bonds are clearly riskier than Treasuries and high-grade municipal bonds because governments ultimately have taxing authority to raise the capital required to repay their debt; corporations clearly don't. Therefore, corporate bonds typically pay higher interest rates, even though the company might ultimately represent the same level of risk as some particular town or government agency.

Logic would insist that maybe it makes more sense to focus on high-grade corporate bonds, where your risk is relatively small and your returns are larger than you'd get with a similarly rated government bond.

Not necessarily so. The tax advantages enjoyed by Treasury and municipal bonds effectively sweetens their rate of return. Or, looked at another way, the taxes you'll pay on the income from the corporate bond works to lower your overall rate of return. This is the tax-equivalent yield, the actual yield you'll earn after taking into account any tax considerations. The higher your tax rate, the greater your tax-equivalent yield on Treasury bonds and particularly muni-bonds. For investors in high-tax jurisdictions such as New York, California, and New Jersey, local municipal bonds will often earn you greater after-tax returns than will corporate bonds with higher interest rates.

Consider this simple example, in which an investor puts money into a $1,000 bond and is subject to a federal tax rate of 35 percent and a state tax rate of 5 percent:

	Corporate	Treasury	Municipal
Interest rate	5%	4.50%	3.75%
Pretax income	$50	$45.00	$37.50
Federal tax due	$17.50	$15.75	
State tax due	$2.50		
After-tax income	$30.00	$29.25	$37.50
Tax-equivalent yield	**3.00%**	**2.93%**	**3.75%**

The municipal bond investor clearly wins out, even though the muni has a decisive interest-rate disadvantage. But taxes play such a defining role in how much of your income remains that they can swing the balance in favor of munis in some instances. Pay attention to that and you can earn fatter returns over time in your bond portfolio.

Guaranteed Return

If the housing-market collapse of 2007 and the stock-market crash of late 2008 rekindled any memories, they were of the Great Depression. As the stock market shed thousands of points over just a few days, and as government officials raced to find solutions that would reverse the tide, the media were filled with stories about the similarities to and differences from the Crash of 1929 and the days of Depression that followed.

In such moments of panic, investors want guaranteed returns, an investment they know will never lose value, and one whose principal will always be there when needed. That desire, though, isn't unique to times of economic disaster. Retirees leaving the workforce for the last time and looking ahead to twenty or more years in retirement ask the same question. Investors who listen to bankers and brokers pitch investment products they're unfamiliar with ask the same question.

The hunt for guaranteed return, however, often conflicts with another key investor want: big returns.

Part of what created the housing collapse and the 2008 stock-market crash was investors—the big institutional players as well as Main Street investors—seeking bigger returns in the late 1990s and early 2000s than they could find in Treasuries and CDs and savings accounts. At a time when those investments were in some cases returning less than 1 percent annually, the prospect of buying a house with nothing down and a 5.75 percent interest rate and renting it out for annualized returns of

(Continued)

8 percent to 10 percent or more seemed brilliant. So, the rationale of the day held, "I won't lose my principal. Besides, housing prices always go up. That's guaranteed." With little more
due diligence than that, investors pulled money from whatever
account they could to buy real estate, in some cases buying
rental property in their IRA, a very risky maneuver, since an IRA
limits the amount of money you can inject into it in a given year,
possibly leaving you unable to afford repairs and other costs for
which you don't have enough money in the account.

Alas, bigger returns walk side by side with bigger risks. You
simply cannot have one without the other. So any investor who
goes in search of big returns that are guaranteed is on a fool's
errand. And any financial professional, or supposed financial
professional, who promises you big returns that are guaranteed
is a fool and should be avoided.

The financial world has but few truly guaranteed returns. I've
mentioned two so far in this book: FDIC-insured bank accounts,
such as savings, money-market accounts, and certificates of
deposit; and Treasury bonds. With any of those, your principal is
as rock solid as principal can possibly get.

Municipal bonds that are insured against default are close to
guaranteed, but in the 2008 stocks-and-housing crisis several
bond insurers struggled, leading many to question what might
happen in a situation in which many municipalities default and
put unexpectedly large strains on insurance agencies.

Annuities, too, would seem to fit the bill, particularly so-
called immediate annuities that begin paying out to you almost
immediately after you sign up. A highly rated insurer such as
Northwestern Mutual has been around since 1857 and will
arguably be around for many years more, giving it a longev-
ity fully capable of living up to its obligations to you. Still, it is
an insurer, and insurers have failed in the past. State guaranty
associations pay claims in the event an insurer fails, but there
are limits to that coverage and you may not recoup your original
principal.

In short, if you unquestionably seek return of principal, not just a return on principal, then settle on bank accounts and Treasury bonds. You won't lose a night's sleep. Just accept the fact, though, that guaranteed returns are guaranteed to be small relative to all the other options around you.

9

Are Mutual Funds and Exchange-Traded Funds for Me?

Why go it alone when you can go alongside many others in the same boat with you?

That's the general concept behind a mutual fund. Few people have the money to buy hundreds of different stocks in one swoop, but many people investing as a single entity do have the necessary resources. This idea of pooling assets to spread the risk among multiple investors who each own proportional amounts of multiple assets dates back to Europe of the 1700s and 1800s, when Dutch, Swiss, and Scottish trustlike vehicles emerged. As the 1900s approached, the concept drifted across the Atlantic and landed in Boston with the Personal Property Trust, America's first closed-end investment fund. But what the world now recognizes as the modern mutual fund has its roots in 1924, when the Massachusetts Investors Trust launched in Boston. From that one fund, the industry in America alone had ballooned by the end of 2008 to more than 8,000 individual funds holding some $12 trillion for investors—just about enough to buy 40,000 Boeing 747 jumbo jets.

For most Americans, mutual funds represent the main means of interacting with Wall Street, typically through a 401(k) plan, maybe an Individual Retirement Account, or through a child's 529

College Savings Plan. In their most basic iteration, mutual funds and their offspring, exchange-traded funds, or ETFs, are simple: With a relatively small initial investment, sometimes as little as $100, you can buy a diversified portfolio holdings scores, if not hundreds, of stocks or bonds or some combination of both. You can track the price every day and buy or sell once a day.

Like to a stock, a mutual fund share represents ownership in a corporation, in this case a corporation that hires managers and analysts and administrative staff who buy and sell and manage a basket of investments for the owners-investors—you. The fund's share price—what's known as the net asset value or NAV—reflects the market value of all the underlying stock owned divided by the number of shares issued by the mutual fund. If a fund has issued one million shares and the value of all the stock the fund company owns is $40 million, the fund's NAV is forty dollars a share.

But mutual funds can be more complicated than a simple commingling of investors' dollars for the purpose of owning many assets in a single fund.

Funds trade in many guises, each concentrating its expertise in a particular corner of the overall investment market. Some funds own only the stocks of big American companies. Some only own small Asian firms. Some buy only healthcare stocks; some, only banks. Some buy shares in markets around the world, some focus solely on Sweden or some other individual country. Some own Treasury bonds, others only high-yield junk bonds or muni-bonds specific to a single state. Some allow you to bet that the Dow Jones Industrial Average is headed lower, some are a leveraged bet that the S&P 500 stock index will move higher.

You also have actively managed and passively managed funds. Actively managed funds employ a portfolio manager, or a team of managers, actively deciding what stocks to buy and sell in the portfolio. Passively managed funds, commonly known as index funds, simply track an index; no active buy and sell decisions are made. If the arbiters or the index decide to remove a stock from the index and replace it with another, then the fund does the same thing, otherwise the portfolio's composition is basically static.

In short, there are mutual funds and ETFs to meet just about any investment need you have or strategy you seek to follow. Indeed, if you never want to own individual stocks and bonds, you can build a well-diversified portfolio of investments by using funds of one shape or another. But here's the statistic to keep in mind: The bulk of mutual fund managers fail to beat the indices against which they benchmark their performance. Among financial facts that aren't very inspiring, that's near the top of the list.

That doesn't mean all mutual fund managers are best avoided. If you don't have the time or inclination to research the stocks and bonds appropriate to your needs, then mutual funds and ETFs are your primary alternatives. Inside most 401(k) and other, similar employer-sponsored retirement-savings plans, they are your only alternative, so it's best you get to know how to pick the best ones you have access to.

After all is said and done, defining "best" among mutual funds is a subjective science because of all the moving parts, not the least of which is the fund's portfolio-management team and its track record at picking winning investments. Managers change jobs with regularity, and a fund that looks like a winner because of its historical returns might begin to suffer once the manager responsible for that performance leaves. Perhaps the best example of that is Fidelity's famed Magellan Fund, once helmed by Peter Lynch, one of the industry's few truly legendary investors. During his thirteen-year tenure, the fund scored returns of nearly 30 percent a year on average, astounding by any measure. After his departure in 1990, Magellan's returns weakened substantially under a series of managers, none of whom was ever able to mirror Lynch's success.

Picking a good mutual fund starts with Morningstar.com, a

website devoted to the minutiae of mutual funds, though you don't need to dig through the minutiae if you don't want to. Though Morningstar is a subscription-based site, the data you most care about is available for free. All you really need to know are the following characteristics:

Strategy: What does the fund invest in and where? Morningstar's "Snapshot" tab defines the category in which a particular fund operates. With the Sequoia Fund, for instance, that category is Large Blend, meaning the fund concentrates on large-company stocks that fit either a value or a growth profile. Value stocks are those that are generally priced cheaply relative to their assets or earnings, while growth stocks are those where the business is growing relatively fast.

On its website Morningstar defines all the various categories it uses to pigeonhole funds.

You want to know a fund's strategy for a simple reason: Does that strategy meet your needs? If all you really want to own is a fund that buys value-oriented, large-company stocks in the United States, then a fund that owns small-company stocks in emerging markets clearly doesn't fit your needs. I'm being dramatic here for effect, since you're not likely to end up with such an extreme example. But you will often have funds to choose from inside 401(k) plans that are very similar in name, or that purport to be one thing though their investments clearly make them something else. The only way to know what you're really buying into is to check out what category each fund falls into before you commit your money.

Performance: The worst tactic you can use when investing in mutual funds is chasing this year's hottest funds. Financial magazines every few months or at least once a year offer a list of the hottest funds you need to own now. What you need to do, instead, is use that magazine for kindling. Racing to own what's already hot means, by definition, you've already missed the big move up.

Academic studies have shown that the hot funds from one year are generally not the hot funds the next year. They cool off, share prices slip, and investors inevitably sell out to dive into the next hot fund, hoping to catch that wave and recoup some of their losses in the previous fund—only to repeat the same cycle. Investors are notorious for buying high amid all the hype and then selling low when the hype dies.

Instead, navigate over to Morningstar's "Total Return" tab and examine a fund's "Performance History" as well as its "Trailing Total Returns." Rather than looking for funds that rate number one in their category, look for those that demonstrate a history of consistently beating the market. In the "Performance History" area, that will show up as "+/– Index" and in the "Total Trailing Returns" area, it's the "+/– S&P 500 TR," both of which detail the fund's performance compared to how well the S&P 500 index fared during the same period.

You're not looking for a mutual-fund manager who shoots the lights out every year. They don't exist. Baseball players who swing for a home run every time at the plate strike out a lot. Same goes for mutual-fund managers who continually swing for fences. When you can buy a low-cost index fund and simply track the S&P 500, why would anyone pay the higher fees associated with an actively managed mutual fund if that manager fails to beat the S&P?

The most successful investors are those who bat for average. They're happy with the consistency of the singles and the doubles, knowing that occasionally they'll get a triple or a home run but not aiming for either.

Also, disregard any returns less than three years old. One-month, year-to-date, and one-year returns are effectively useless. You want to see how a fund has performed over different economic cycles, which means you want to see performance data over three, five, and ten years. Anything less is just a hiccup.

Management team: As I noted a few pages back, managers mean a lot to an actively managed mutual fund, since their decisions directly affect the portfolio's overall returns.

Morningstar's "Snapshot" page indicates how long the current manager or team has been in place. The "Management" page provides greater detail on the manager's investment history.

Essentially, you want to know that the manager in charge of your fund is the manager responsible for the track record. If you find a fund with a great track record, but a spanking-new manager, you can't be sure that the strategies that generated those returns are still in place. Best to hold off and wait for that manager to build a track record.

Fees: How much you pay to own a fund is a crucial factor. The annual fees you pay reduce the amount of return the fund generates, since the costs of running the fund come out of the returns it earns.

Funds either charge a "load" or are "no-load." A load is the fee you pay to buy into the fund. A front-end load means you're paying a fee up front, so that a 4 percent load on an initial $1,000 investment means that only $960 is actually going to work for you; the fund company keeps the other $40 as the fee. A back-end load, or deferred load, means you pay the fee when you exit the fund based on the amount of assets you're drawing out. If your $1,000 investment grows to $2,000 and you have a 2 percent back-end load, you're paying $40 again and bringing back home the remaining $1,960. A level-load fund charges an ongoing load every year.

No-load funds charge fees, too, much like a level-load fund. They're called 12b-1 fees that the fund uses for advertising and marketing purposes. This fee can't be more than 0.25 percent of your assets under management with the fund company.

Investors have been trained by the financial media to flee load-based mutual funds in a Pavlovian rejection of fees. Some loads are certainly onerous and deserving of derision. But tarring them all can be highly shortsighted. If a manager has proven his worth by consistently outperforming the fund's benchmark, and has outperformed peers in the same category, then the fees are rather beside the point. The First Eagle Overseas Fund is a prime example. The fund plays in the small- and midsized foreign-company category, an area where manager expertise clearly adds value, since researching small companies overseas is a challenging process. First Eagle charges a deferred load of 1 percent of your assets. Some investors will balk at that when they can go off and find a no-load fund with a similar focus.

However, under the guidance of Jean-Marie Eveillard, a legendary international-fund manager, the First Eagle Overseas Fund has consistently outperformed its benchmark index and has routinely ranked among the very top small- and midsized foreign-company funds. Such funds can be worth the cost because the returns you earn are better than you would have received elsewhere.

What you want to pay attention to on the Morningstar site is the "Fees & Expenses" tab, which shows the net expense ratio. This is the total, annual cost to you, the amount of money you will pay to the fund company based on your assets under management.

Net expenses vary widely. But you can typically find good, actively managed funds with expense ratios below 1 percent. That will sneak somewhat higher with foreign-focused funds, up toward 1.5 percent or so, because of the added costs of transacting business overseas and conducting the necessary research.

Index funds will be dramatically lower, since the administrative costs are so much less. You'll find some, particularly Vanguard and Fidelity index funds, that charge as little as 0.1 percent to 0.25 percent.

When you mix all these traits together, you are effectively looking for a fund that generates some of the most consistent long-term returns, at a cost lower than its peers, and with a management team that has been around for a while. You'll notice I skipped strategy. That's up to you and your needs. Telling you to go buy a small-company stock fund because they perform well historically is pointless if you don't want the risk and volatility inherent in small-company stocks.

Once you determine your needs (and I'll offer some advice on asset allocation in Chapter 17), it's just a matter of spending a little time examining the mutual fund options available to you and picking those that best meet the criteria I described above.

I will say this, though: By and large, index funds and ETFs are the most cost-effective ways to build a portfolio and are especially useful for investors who don't want to worry about which fund manager is better than another and which fund has the best returns.

Index funds, as the name implies, track some particular index of stocks or bonds or commodities. Vanguard's 500 Index Fund, for instance, shadows the S&P 500. Fidelity's U.S. Bond Index Fund mimics the Lehman Brothers U.S. Aggregate Bond Index.

Index funds are typically passive, meaning no portfolio managers are making active decisions to buy Merck today and sell Microsoft tomorrow. The fund owns whatever is in the particular index it's designed to follow. If the arbiters of the S&P 500 Index decide to replace one of the 500 component stocks, then any index fund built to perform alongside the S&P 500 will do the same inside its portfolio.

ETFs operate almost identically, but with one significant caveat. They constantly trade during the day. You can buy and sell an ETF at any moment, giving you the benefit of up-to-the-second price and instant liquidity, should you decide you want in or out during the trading day. Mutual funds, by comparison, price just once a day, after the market closes. If you want to buy or sell a mutual fund, you place your order during the day and the transaction is complete after the fund prices at the end of the day. The downside is that you aren't sure what price you'll get for the fund until after the transaction is compete.

These days, you have an abundance of index funds and ETFs to choose from. You can start with a basic S&P 500 fund and a generic bond-index fund as your core, and then layer on everything from an index fund tracking international real estate, to one that follows the currency movements of the Mexican peso, to funds that follow U.S. cotton prices and the comparatively prosaic S&P 600 Index of small-company U.S. stocks. And in between that narrow list are hundreds of other options. You can even find ETFs that bet on falling prices in some particular index if you happen to be bearish on the market or some narrow corner of the market.

My point is that you can build a wide-ranging and highly diversified portfolio simply owning index mutual funds and ETFs. And perhaps their strongest suit is that they're generally cheaper than actively managed funds. Vanguard 500 Index Fund, for example, charges just 0.15 percent a year, or $1.50 a year per $1,000 under management.

The risk in owning index funds and ETFs is that you forsake any potential outperformance. After all, index funds are designed to mirror the index, not outrun it. Then again, you won't do markedly worse than the index either in periods when the underlying assets are falling in value. Actively managed funds run the risk of doing substantially worse, and many do.

If all you seek is performance generally equal to some market as a whole, an index fund is a solid, cost-effective choice.

10

What About Options, Futures, and Gold?

The goal of any portfolio is to mitigate risk by spreading your assets across multiple classes of investments. Investors often concentrate on the key trio—stocks, bonds, and cash. And for most, some combination of those three offers most of the necessary diversity.

Other asset classes exist, though some are more exotic than others, and many are too risky for average investors to play with. Some assets require a great deal of babysitting, lest you get burned. Options and futures are two such investments. Both can be quite useful for reducing risk in your overall portfolio—or even adding risk, if you're a gambler—but each also requires that you watch your positions like a hawk, necessitating a level of supervision you might not have time for in your daily life.

Options and futures are contracts that mandate you buy or sell at a predetermined price a particular stock or commodity at some point in the future. Options cover stocks and stock-market indices. Futures cover commodities ranging from gold to frozen orange juice, corn to currencies. Unlike stocks or bonds or mutual funds, however, options and futures contracts are decaying assets. Every day that passes takes a day off the life of your contract. That means you can't invest and then sit on paper losses until a recovery happens. While that might work with stocks, with futures and options the contracts could expire long before a price recovery ever arrives. Most expire between three months and two years.

Both options and futures can be used conservatively (to hedge against losses) or aggressively (to gamble on the movement of some stock, index, or commodity). Farmers, for instance, routinely buy and sell futures to protect against price moves in the crops they grow. This helps preserve their income if the market for their crop moves away from them. Wall Street traders, meanwhile, who clearly aren't out farming the crops, might buy and sell the same futures contract purely on a bet that the crop price will rise or fall. The farmer is trading conservatively; the trader, aggressively.

The benefit and risk of options and futures is the leverage you employ.

Options

In the options market, each contract typically represents 100 shares of the underlying stock. A single contract on Wal-Mart covers 100 shares of the stock. These Wal-Mart options trade as either "puts" or "calls."

A put allows the contract owner to sell, or put, to another investor 100 shares of a particular company at a set price on or before a set date.

A call allows the contract owner to buy, or call, from another investor 100 shares of a particular company at a set price on or before a set date.

The contracts are substantially more complex that that, though. For not only can you be the contract's owner, the one who originally bought the contract, you can also be the contract's seller. By definition, every option represents a buyer and a seller—effectively a bull and a bear—tied to each other for the duration of the option's lifespan. As the price moves, the two sides of the trade move in opposite directions.

Let's look at a relatively simple options trade so you can see the action and understand what's happening on both sides of the ledger. I'll pick on Wal-Mart again, just because it's a big company everyone likely knows. And I'll explain this from the bullish and bearish viewpoints. As I write this in October 2008, Wal-Mart's stock trades at $53.25.

The bullish case: You may expect Wal-Mart shares to surge past $60 by the end of the year. Wal-Mart's 08 Dec $60 calls (giving you the right to buy 100 shares of Wal-Mart at $60 per share by December 20, 2008) were trading on this day at $1.50, meaning you're paying $1.50 per share to buy that contract. Your cost, therefore, is $150 per contract to cover the 100-share count each contract represents.

The bearish case: You may expect Wal-Mart won't get anywhere near $60 by the end of the year. So you take the opposite side of this trade, selling those call contracts to the buyer. In doing so, this buyer pays into your account that $150 for each contract. You now have an obligation to sell 100 shares of Wal-Mart if the stock closes above $60.

Potential outcome number one: Wal-Mart meets the bull's expectations and races to $65 by the end of the year. The bull has two choices: Sell the contract, which will have increased in value to reflect the fact that Wal-Mart's share price exceeds the contract's $60 exercise price, or if you want to own the stock, exercise the contract directly and buy those 100 shares at $60. The purchase price goes to the bear, who sold the contract to initiate this trade in the first place. Your total cost to own Wal-Mart is the $60 per share for the stock, plus the $1.50 per share you originally paid for the option—or a total of $61.50 a share. (You might wonder why not just buy the stock at $53.25. Two reasons: First, options allow you to control more shares for fewer dollars; in this case you can spend $5,235 to control 100 shares, or $150 to control that same 100 shares. So, options provide leverage. And second, you reduce your risk. If you're concerned Wal-Mart might instead fall in value, then your only risk is the $150 you spent on the option, not hundreds or even thousands if the shares fall precipitously.)

The bear is a loser in this case, and has two options as well: Buy back the contract to negate his obligation of having to supply 100 shares of Wal-Mart, though the cost of the contract will be substantially higher than where he originally sold it because the stock price has risen above the exercise price; or pony up the 100 shares of Wal-Mart stock. If the bear owns the shares, they're pulled from his account and transferred to the bull, and in return the bear receives $6,000, the $60 per share contract price for each of the 100 shares. In the worst case, the bear has to go into the market and buy those 100 shares of Wal-Mart for $65 each. The bear's loss is the $65 price to buy the stock, minus the $61.50 the bull has paid—or a total loss of $3.50 a share.

Potential outcome number two: Wal-Mart fails to reach $60 by the expiration date. For the bull, the contract expires worthless. After all, no one's going to spend $60 on a share of Wal-Mart when those shares are trading for less than that in the market. The bull's loss is the $150 contract price.

The bear is the winner. He doesn't have to supply the 100 shares of Wal-Mart. Instead, he gets to keep the $150 contract price the bull originally paid.

Identical processes are at work with put options, only in reverse. The buyer of a put is the bear betting that Wal-Mart's stock is headed lower, and is paying for the right to sell 100 shares to a bull who thinks the stock will rally. In this case, the bear is paying to own that contract. If the stock falls below the exercise price, the bear puts those 100 shares to the bull, who is contractually obligated to pay the exercise price. If the stock rises, the contract expires worthless and the bear has lost the initial cost of buying the contract.

The bull is the seller of the contract this time around, taking in the money the bear is paying. In essence, the bull is betting Wal-Mart's shares will rise. If it does, the contract will expire worth-less, leaving the bull to keep the premium the bear paid. If the price falls, the bull is contractually obligated to buy the shares at the higher price, or, before that happens, buy back the contract at an elevated amount.

Options strategies are too numerous to detail. And while many online brokerage and options-trading firms litter the Internet these days offering ultra-low cost trades, options are best left to those who do it for a living. This isn't an area where Main Street inves-tors should stalk returns. While some strategies can be conserva-tive, missteps can lead to unlimited losses in some cases.

Futures

Futures falls into the same category. Futures contracts are time-sensitive, and if the price of corn or hog bellies or gold moves oppo-site to your expectations, your contract is sunk and you've lost your capital.

But that doesn't mean you should avoid the commodities under-lying futures contracts. There's a place for them in a balanced portfolio.

Commodities don't necessarily move in conjunction with other assets, though sometimes they clearly do. More often commodities move based on supply and demand. A drought dries out Australia and that country's wheat crop shrivels, affecting global supply, and demand continues rising for wheat-based products in the devel-oped and developing world. Rising demand, falling supply—prices go up.

In broad terms, demand for all kinds of commodities is on the rise, though in periods of recession that demand can slip tempo-rarily, as witnessed in the 2008 financial crisis when oil and gold and copper and wheat and other commodities fell in price. Step back, though, and take a longer view of time. World population is on the rise and major nations such as India, China, Brazil, and Russia are rapidly developing their economies, a process in which their citizens are growing wealthier and increasingly moving into cities.

This combination of rising wealth and increasing urbanization puts big strains on world commodities. Wealthier people eat better and different foods, such as beef, dairy, chicken, and pork, all of which adds to the demand for grains. They shop for better clothing, increasing demand for cotton as well as for the chemicals necessary for man-made fibers like rayon and polyester. Urbanization draws ever-larger numbers of people out of rural settings and places them in metropolitan centers, where they find jobs that provide greater income, leading to those changing dietary and clothing demands, and requiring countries to construct the infrastructure needed for urban living—roads, bridges, hospitals, schools, shopping centers, office towers, train stations, airports, zoos. All that construction consumes the ores that go into steel; the minerals and metals necessary for the wiring that goes into cables and telecommunications links; the oil and coal and natural gas that fire the power plants to provide electricity.

You can't easily buy exposure to all the various commodities that benefit from a growing world. But you should have some exposure, because commodities as an asset class are lightly correlated with stocks and bonds, meaning commodity prices generally don't move in tandem with either. That's good for your portfolio because it means commodities can balance out the volatility inherent in stock and bond prices.

The way to invest in commodities, however, is through a mutual fund or ETF that specifically targets this sector. I won't give you advice on which one to buy, because books are inherently dated when you read them, and while a specific fund might make sense as I'm writing this, it may not be a good option when you're reading it. Instead, I encourage you to use the free research options at Morningstar.com and ETFconnect.com, both of which provide an abundance of up-to-date data on all mutual funds and ETFs.

Don't overload your portfolio, though, with commodities. You don't need much more than about 5 percent or 10 percent of your money in a commodities fund.

Gold

Finally, there's gold. Technically, it's a commodity, since it is one of the mined metals, just like copper or silver or nickel. In practical terms, however, gold is its own asset class and often trades as the ultimate currency. In the earliest chapters of Genesis, Abram is described as "very rich in cattle, in silver, and in gold," and in the final chapters of Revelation, the new Jerusalem is described as having a street of pure gold. Gold has represented a store of value and the ultimate prosperity since biblical times.

Today it maintains that same role. For investors and savers, gold represents wealth no country can control. While governments can impose a value on their currency by altering monetary policy and through national laws, they have little power to dictate the price of gold, which trades in the global marketplace on the basis of supply and demand fundamentals. For that reason, many cultures still accumulate wealth through gold, and in some cultures women give to their husbands a dowry of gold.

The metal was once the cornerstone of global finance. As early as the late seventeenth century, gold backed national currencies. At various points in time, currencies from the British pound to the Swiss franc, the U.S. dollar, the Japanese yen, and the Russian ruble, among others, were all backed by gold, and note-holders could trade their paper money for an equivalent sum of gold.

Nowadays, every currency in the world is a fiat currency, its value as a means of trade authorized only because a governmental body says that piece of paper is worth something, though no physical assets support that claim or the currency's purported value. That could prove a real problem for the U.S. dollar in coming years, and is a fine reason why every portfolio should include exposure to gold.

U.S. economic policy is killing the value of the American dollar. U.S. governmental debts, the amount of money we owe to creditors, are so large, at more than $10 trillion in November 2008, that repayment seems nigh impossible. The federal budget for 2008 overshot expectations by a record $438 billion, and that was before officials started draining the $700 billion fund to repair the damage caused by the credit crisis and started doling out hundreds of billions more for other crash-inspired crises. As I write this, expectations are that the budget deficit for 2009 will top $500 billion. Just to top it off, there are the looming fiscal woes of Social Security and Medicare, two of the largest entitlement programs that are consuming increasingly larger portions of the federal budget.

To make payments on all these obligations, the government will effectively be left with one option: print money. The more you print, though, the more you risk either consumer price inflation or asset price inflation, which is what helped lead to the 2008 crash.

We could reduce the deficit by reducing our consumption, meaning we buy fewer goods from overseas suppliers, while at the same time increasing the amount of goods we make that head overseas. But the United States is increasingly a consumption-based, service-oriented economy. We seem almost incapable of pursuing the Good Life without credit, and the services we provide are not something you can ship to a foreign country. Tax rates can rise, which will allow the Treasury to collect more dollars to repay the debt, and that's a real possibility at some point.

Or, the government can allow the dollar to shrivel against

world currencies. Doing so makes the goods America does sell overseas cheaper, causing foreigners to buy more American goods, thereby reducing the trade imbalance. It also means the government can repay its debts with depreciated currency, making the deficit not seem so large.

That's not good for American households, though. A weak dollar makes foreign goods more expensive here at home—and don't think you can escape that by only buying American. Much of what you buy in daily life has all or parts of its origin somewhere overseas. Rising prices at home can lead to overall inflation.

However you look at it, gold is primed to shine.

While the U.S. dollar remains, even in its current weakened state, the currency of last resort (see the upcoming sidebar), gold is the final store of value. If global citizens ever lose faith in world currencies, for whatever reason, gold will likely stand as the internationally recognized symbol of value, much as currencies do today.

Unlike wheat and oil and other such commodities, gold is easy to store in physical form in a bank safe-deposit box or a family safe or lockbox. Coin stores and bullion shops sell everything from a single gram of gold to a kilo-sized bar to one-ounce gold coins from the United States, China, Canada, and Australia, among others. If you don't want to own the physical asset because of risk of loss or theft, many ETFs either track gold prices or physically own shares of gold in secured, limited-access bank vaults.

Gold generally rises in value when economic or geopolitical tensions rise. Those are the moments when concerns about financial security spur savers to turn some of their dollars or pounds or yen into gold, expecting that if currencies fall in value, their pieces of gold will rise in value to help preserve their financial self-sufficiency. Gold is also a primary inflation hedge, since, as a hard asset, it rises in value alongside other hard assets, such as real estate or cases of the finest French Bordeaux.

Whether or not you believe in gold as a store of value, a balanced portfolio should have some exposure to the metal, if only as an insurance policy against economic Armageddon or, less beastly, a bout of sustained inflation that eats away at your purchasing power. The rise in gold prices will help offset those escalating costs. As with commodities in general, 5 percent or 10 percent of your portfolio in gold is sufficient.

The Greenback

Though it boldly carries "The United States of America" across its face, the U.S. dollar is most assuredly the world's currency. Nearly two-thirds of America's banknotes circulate overseas. Every major commodity the world trades, particularly oil, is priced in dollars. And any time turmoil roils the landscape—from financial panic to war—the dollar stands as the beacon of security because whether they live in a central London apartment or a dirt-floor hut in a central African village, investors, traders, merchants, and savers girdling the globe hold the U.S. dollar, the greenback, as the safest currency in the world.

If you think of a country as a corporation, then its currency is the corporation's stock. When underlying fundamentals are strong, everyone wants to own the stock. When the fundamentals are weak, investors bail out.

Bailing out is exactly what investors have been doing with the U.S. dollar. Since the early 2000s, the greenback has lost value against nearly every major currency in the world. The 2008 crisis temporarily slowed the fall because, returning to the safety factor, panicked investors the world over rushed to own the greenback to protect their finances as stocks, bonds, real estate, and other assets plunged in value from Auckland to Hong Kong, Johannesburg to London to New York.

That situation promises to change when the crisis passes and investors refocus on the dollar's underlying fundamentals.

What will they see? Fundamental flaws that threaten to undermine the greenback. For that reason, prudence says you should diversify away from exposure solely to dollar-based assets to ward against longer-term weakness in the U.S. currency.

U.S. trade and budget deficits are at gargantuan proportions. Worse is the fact that the situation can only deteriorate, because two massive federal programs, Social Security and Medicare, consume a vast portion of the federal budget and are careening toward a financial disaster. Each is ill-funded, and politicians have shown no fortitude in tackling the problem even as the population of recipients promises to explode as baby boomers retire in vast numbers.

On top of that, politicians have layered onto the budget an exceedingly costly Middle East war.

The financial bailout in 2008 has been estimated by analysts at CNBC to total an astounding $4.28 trillion—more than the cost of World War II! To put such a large number into perspective, the M1 money supply, the supply of liquid cash floating through the economy, was slightly less than $1.4 trillion as of this writing. Though some of those bailout dollars are theoretically to be repaid, that proof is still in the offing.

In the meantime, to meet the necessary payments, the government must borrow ever-larger sums of money by auctioning off Treasury obligations, the U.S. government's IOUs, to investors around the world who are using their savings to fund our profligacy and our promises to retirees. We, of course, must repay what we borrow as a nation, adding to the overall cost of our debt. The interest expense on our national debt for the 2008 fiscal year amounted to $451 billion—a meager $14,306 per second. If government can't borrow enough money, it can always crank up the Treasury's printing presses and simply print additional dollars, adding to the global supply of dollars, which, over time, breeds inflation, potentially rampant inflation.

All of this debt, all of the federal funding obligations hurtling

(Continued)

at us, and all these excess dollars flooding the market ultimately weakens the dollar relative to other currencies. As the dollar weakens, the cost of living rises in America because so much of what we buy comes from overseas, including a great deal of the oil we consume.

One way to protect against a devalued dollar is to own the currencies against which the dollar is falling. Currencies trade in pairs in a see-saw action; as one falls in value, the other necessarily rises. So if the dollar is down, then the euro, the yen, the Canadian dollar, and others are up. If you own those other currencies, your dollar losses are offset by equal profits on the other side.

Exposure to foreign currencies comes through owning foreign stocks or bonds, either directly or in an international mutual fund, though that strategy subjects you to corporate and systemic stock-market risk, or the risk that a company or a stock market will run into trouble. A less risky strategy is to own savings accounts or CDs denominated in any of the major currencies. You won't find these on offer at your local bank and trust. Instead, you'll need to go online, to Internet-based banks such as EverBank.com, one of a very limited number of banks offering foreign-currency accounts in the United States. EverBank's CDs and savings accounts cover a variety of currencies, from the euro and British pound to the South African rand and the Chinese renminbi.

These accounts are FDIC protected, though you still face the possibility of loss. If the bank were to fail, the FDIC would return to you the value of your account. However, your account value could be less than your original investment if the currency you select falls in value against the dollar. Since there are so many Internet bank scams, you should verify with an outside source that the Internet bank is legitimate and is FDIC insured.

Along with protecting you from a falling dollar, a key benefit of a foreign-currency account is the opportunity to earn greater returns on your money. At a time when the average one-year,

U.S.-dollar CD returns about 3.6 percent a year, a New Zealand dollar CD at EverBank offered a rate of 5.75 percent. The South African rand offered 9 percent for six months. I am not specifically advocating the NZ dollar or the rand; I'm just pointing out that higher-yielding opportunities exist.

No matter what currency you own, you run the risk that your target currency fall in value against the dollar, potentially undercutting the interest-rate return you earn, or even wiping it out completely and leading to capital losses. Yet if the currency strengthens, you get the double-sided benefit of a meatier interest rate and capital gains that will help offset the impact on your portfolio or your lifestyle that a falling dollar can have.

If you do seek to pursue foreign-currency exposure, avoid currency-trading accounts. They're all over the Internet these days and allow you to open an account with as little as $100. They also allow you to employ an abundance of leverage, in some cases letting you control $400 for every dollar on deposit, so that with a $100 initial balance you can trade $40,000 worth of currency at any one time.

Such leverage can work in your favor if the market is moving with you, but such leverage can also wipe you out in just minutes if currency moves swing against you. And in this case, "swinging against you" can mean a currency movement that's measured in just fractions of a penny.

Stick to foreign-currency CDs and savings accounts. Profits won't be nearly as large if the currency moves with you, but you will still have a relatively large percentage of your cash remaining if it moves against you.

11

Is Homeownership a Love Nest or Money Pit?

We all know the script, the long-running story of America in which we're all in pursuit of a home, a piece of property to call our own, where each of us can dig around in the dirt and remake a collection of wood and brick and stucco into our personal version of the American Dream.

It is pure Americana, defining success for many of us, that "I've made it!" moment, regardless of whether the structure is a mansion in a well-groomed ZIP code or a small, shotgun house in a modest neighborhood. Our home is our haven from the storms of daily life—a place where we feel safe; where we reunite with our family for daily meals and special occasions; where we celebrate and mourn; where life is created and where life sometimes passes.

Because homeownership is so central to our aspirations, and because the costs ripple so deeply through our daily finances, this chapter focuses on the fundamentals you need to know to become a savvy consumer of real estate services. And I'll start by offering a warning: The American Dream can easily transform into a nightmare for those who have the mistaken notion that they deserve what they want now rather than what they can actually afford. In such cases, owning a home can be a private hell that grips your wallet and your personal life.

The events of 2008 demonstrated the downside of home-buying

all too profoundly, as discussed in the opening pages of this book.

Clearly, homeownership doesn't regularly result in such a dramatic chain of events. Yet, on a much smaller, more personal scale, individual bankruptcies and foreclosures happen routinely, in good economies and bad, because of faulty decisions made before buying a house. This chapter aims to help you avoid that fate. It aims to help you find the Love Nest, while evading the disastrous Money Pit.

Should You Even Buy: Renting versus Owning

Not everyone is meant to be a homeowner, despite the platitudes of politicians pandering to voters. That's not a slight against any particular group of people, and it's not to imply that the American Dream is off limits to certain classes. It merely means that some people do not possess the necessary financial strength to own a house at the moment they seek to own it, even if a bank is willing to provide a mortgage. And that's not a bad thing. Knowing your finances can't support a particular want is a sign of a financial wisdom and restraint that will serve you well in life.

Buying a home is more than the cost of the house. Each year requires the payment of property taxes. Protection against hurricanes, tornadoes, fire, theft, and other calamities necessitates homeowner's—and sometimes, federal flood—insurance. Homeowners' associations might want several hundred to a few thousand dollars annually to pay for common-area upkeep. Through the years, you must repaint or reside your house, replace the roof, repair broken or aging appliances, pay for landscaping or provide the manpower yourself. Those costs can add thousands of dollars a year to the principal and interest payments you send to the bank every month. An inability to afford those costs can pressure your financial life and cause much strain in your relationships.

Of course, renting isn't without its costs, too—some financial, some psychic. Catastrophe coverage in the form of renter's insurance is a must, unless you relish replacing all your goods in a disaster. Though your monthly rent might be less than someone's mortgage for an equal amount of space, rent is susceptible to inflation increases imposed by landlords on a regular basis, while a fixed-rate mortgage isn't. Thus, rent can exceed tax-adjusted mortgage payments in just a few years. You don't always have your space, hard-pressed as you are against other units in a building, privy to their privacies when you really don't want to be. You're not methodically building up equity that you can tap later in life if needed.

Adherents argue their respective side of the debate with equal aplomb and passion. And they're both right. But the truth is that there's no universally applicable answer to the question of which is the smarter option. Choosing between the two possibilities is a facts-and-circumstances exercise: The facts and circumstances specific to *your* life will help you determine which approach benefits *you* best, regardless of what your friends and your uncle and your coworkers insist.

A house can certainly be a great investment, even if accidentally. Home prices generally rise over time, so your monthly mortgage payments will systematically fatten your net worth over time. Just as clearly, though, a rental can seem a brilliant move for those who don't want to be burdened with the costs of homeownership, who would rather invest their money in other assets, and who relish the freedom to move around unencumbered by the relative permanency of a house.

The question you have to ask yourself is this: Am I a renter or a homeowner? *Homeowners are people who:*

- want to own a physical asset as an investment in real estate, whether that's a condo, a city apartment, or a single-family home, a duplex or a fourplex on a piece of land;
- seek the freedom to remodel the house or landscape the yard

to match their specific tastes without having to worry about what a landlord might say;

- don't mind managing the upkeep of their property, everything from painting to mowing;
- are okay with limited mobility, since you generally can't vacate on a moment's notice;
- want to build equity over time, or see rent as money that lines someone else's pocket;
- recognize that tax benefits mean the government is effectively helping them buy some portion of their home.

Renters are people who:

- have no interest in owning a piece of physical property;
- are thrilled that the landlord is responsible for everything from maintenance to broken toilets or a wind-damaged roof;
- want nothing to do with a mortgage because it limits their mobility;
- would rather invest their money in savings or stocks or a retirement plan than in building real estate equity;
- are concerned houses in their particular city or in some particular economic period are overvalued, and buying would mean risking your down payment if prices were to tumble.

Three Key Myths about Renting and Home Buying

Myth 1: Renting equals "throwing your money away."

Nonsense. Renting is effectively paying for a service rendered. Everyone has to live somewhere, and renters are simply paying for the shelter, not all those extraneous costs of homeownership (of

(Continued)

course, a person renting a property needs to recover his costs, so a tenant must be careful to have spelled out in a lease agreement what expenses or repairs he is or is not liable for). A mortgage is effectively rent, too—you're just renting from yourself.

True, you build equity paying off a mortgage, but renting can be a cheaper alternative when you factor in all those annual costs of homeownership. A renter could calculate the cost differential between buying and renting and use that savings to invest—as well as the money that otherwise would have funded the down payment on the house. (To be fair, the profits on those investments would be taxed to some degree, and the profits on the sale of your house would, as of this writing, escape taxation up to $250,000 for a single tax filer or $500,000 for a married couple.)

Likewise, you could argue that buying means "throwing your money away" on all those items that do not add monetary value to our property, such as the costs of obtaining the mortgage or selling the house, the property taxes and insurance you pay each month, or the mortgage interest. Then there are all the maintenance and upkeep costs that keep the house presentable but do not increase its value. Add them up and they might just exceed the rent you'd otherwise pay. If nothing else, those costs will greatly reduce the benefits.

Myth 2: Home prices always go up.
Another way to phrase this might be, "Houses are a good investment." But I refer you to the events of 2007 and 2008 mentioned already. Home prices can and do fall, sometimes with great speed and depth, as they have in such places as Miami, San Diego, Las Vegas, and Boston. Moreover, home prices can and do stagnate, as many Rust Belt communities have found.

Real estate prices do not always go up, and when they fall hard, a home can be a horrendous investment that wipes out the original equity you employed to buy the property in the first place.

Myth 3: Tax benefits make homeownership a no-brainer.

That's not always true. Real estate tax benefits are tied to your income bracket, so that if you're in, for instance, the 25 percent bracket, you can deduct twenty-five cents of every dollar paid in mortgage interest. But even that isn't necessarily a benefit unavailable to renters. Every taxpayer is allowed a "standard deduction," and if your mortgage interest and other deductions combined don't exceed the standard deduction, then you'll see no tax benefit in owning instead of renting.

Moreover, if you do pay more in mortgage interest than you're eligible for in the standard deduction, the only tax advantage you hold over the renter is the difference between the mortgage interest you pay and the size of that standard deduction. So, for instance, the standard deduction for 2009 is projected at about $11,400 for a married couple filing jointly. Assume your mortgage interest for the year is $12,000. Your tax benefit is calculated off that $600 difference, and that won't be a tremendous advantage.

Regardless of which side of the rent-versus-buy debate you ultimately fall on, this much is true: Homeowners tend to accumulate greater wealth than do renters. That fact comes courtesy of the Federal Reserve. The agency has routinely found in its Survey of Consumer Finances that homeowners are richer than renters, and that holds up across all manner of income brackets, from wealthy to working-class.

The reasons are simple. First, buying a house is the equivalent of consistent, forced savings, since a portion of every mortgage payment increases the amount of equity you own in your home. Renters are tempted to take on the habits of the general population, who often shirk consistent savings. In the overly, and overtly, consumerist culture that has become America, we do not think in terms of preparing for tomorrow when so many shiny baubles capture our attention today, consuming the discretionary income that could help build wealth.

Second, despite the fact that home prices can fall, historically they rise over time, generally at or slightly above the rate of inflation. While you will spend money on property taxes, insurance, maintenance, and the like, and while those costs will eat into your ultimate returns, your home's price appreciation will likely exceed those expenses and you will come out ahead.

The great benefit of this long-term price appreciation is that it happens in a leveraged environment. When you borrow to buy a house, you typically put down 20 percent of the purchase price, in turn allowing you to benefit from price movements tied to a much larger asset. On a $200,000 home, you put down, say, $40,000. A decade later the house is worth about $270,000, assuming home prices increase at roughly 3 percent a year. Sell the house and that original $40,000 is now $110,000—and that doesn't include the thousands in increased equity you'll have from the 120 mortgage payments you will have mailed to the lender. The bottom line is that a 35 percent total increase in the value of your home nearly triples the value of your original down payment. That's leverage for you.

12

Will I Be a Homeowner?

Statistically speaking, homeownership is in your future. Housing market studies conducted by government agencies show that about 90 percent of Americans will own a house at some point between the ages of twenty and ninety. Too many, unfortunately, do not understand what they're signing up for, relying on others to tell them what they can and can't afford, and allowing their heartstrings to manipulate their purse strings, often to the detriment of their personal finances. I want to help you avoid that before you even begin pursuing that American Dream.

The Mortgage

Despite vernacular use, a mortgage is not a "home loan." It a legal document you give to a lender, pledging your property as collateral in exchange for the cash needed to complete the purchase of your home. The mortgage protects the lender, giving it the right to foreclose on and sell your property to recoup the unpaid debt you owe. A mortgage can either be recourse or nonrecourse. In the first case, the lender has rights against all your assets. In the second, the lender's only security is the house. You obviously want to go "nonrecourse." Many homeowners today find that their mortgage exceeds the value of the home, and regrettably they mail in the keys and walk away.

Three numbers define every mortgage: principal, interest rate, and duration.

Principal: The sum of money a lender provides to help you purchase a home.

Interest: The annual rate charged on the principal for providing you the use of the money.

Duration: The amount of time you have to repay the mortgage, traditionally between fifteen and thirty years.

With this trio, you can calculate exactly what your monthly principal-and-interest cost will be for any house. This way you will know if you really can afford a particular home before you grow too attached to the idea of buying it. Remember, though, that this principal-and-interest payment marks only a portion of your total monthly cost. Property taxes and insurance are both mandatory, as well, and are often lumped into the mortgage payment. To gain a truer picture of the cost of a particular home, ask your insurance agent for a rough guide to insuring houses in the price range and ZIP codes you're looking at (rates can change depending on a home's location within a city), and ask your real estate agent to provide property tax data for each house you like.

Calculating principal and interest is quite easy on any computer spreadsheet. With Microsoft's Excel, for instance, type into three neighboring cells the three key numbers—the principal borrowed, the interest rate a lender is charging, and the duration of the mortgage.

In a fourth cell, plug in Excel's payment function, the so-called PMT function, which you can find by using the "Help" icon if you aren't familiar with Excel. The spreadsheet will instantly calculate your monthly costs and will allow you to change all the variables so that you can examine the impact on your wallet of a higher or lower purchase price, a higher or lower interest rate, and a longer or shorter duration.

To save you a little effort when shopping for a home, use the chart below. It shows the monthly costs for each $1,000 mort-

MORTGAGE CALCULATOR

Rate	15-year	30-year	Rate	15-year	30-year
3%	$6.91	$4.22	6.25%	$8.57	$6.16
3.125%	$6.97	$4.28	6.375%	$8.64	$6.24
3.25%	$7.03	$4.35	6.50%	$8.71	$6.32
3.375%	$7.09	$4.42	6.625%	$8.78	$6.40
3.50%	$7.15	$4.49	6.75%	$8.85	$6.49
3.625%	$7.21	$4.56	6.875%	$8.92	$6.57
3.75%	$7.27	$4.63	7%	$8.99	$6.65
3.875%	$7.33	$4.70	7.125%	$9.06	$6.74
4%	$7.40	$4.77	7.25%	$9.13	$6.82
4.125%	$7.46	$4.85	7.375%	$9.20	$6.91
4.25%	$7.52	$4.92	7.50%	$9.27	$6.99
4.375%	$7.59	$4.99	7.625%	$9.34	$7.08
4.50%	$7.65	$5.07	7.75%	$9.41	$7.16
4.625%	$7.71	$5.14	7.875%	$9.48	$7.25
4.75%	$7.78	$5.22	8%	$9.56	$7.34
4.875%	$7.84	$5.29	8.125%	$9.63	$7.42
5%	$7.91	$5.37	8.25%	$9.70	$7.51
5.125%	$7.97	$5.44	8.375%	$9.77	$7.60
5.25%	$8.04	$5.52	8.50%	$9.85	$7.69
5.375%	$8.10	$5.60	8.625%	$9.92	$7.78
5.50%	$8.17	$5.68	8.75%	$9.99	$7.87
5.625%	$8.24	$5.76	8.875%	$10.07	$7.96
5.75%	$8.30	$5.84	9%	$10.14	$8.05
5.875%	$8.37	$5.92	9.125%	$10.22	$8.14
6%	$8.44	$6.00	9.25%	$10.29	$8.23
6.125%	$8.51	$6.08	9.375%	$10.37	$8.32

(Continued)

MORTGAGE CALCULATOR *(Continued)*

Rate	15-year	30-year	Rate	15-year	30-year
9.50%	$10.44	$8.41	10.25%	$10.90	$8.96
9.625%	$10.52	$8.50	10.375%	$10.98	$9.05
9.75%	$10.59	$8.59	10.50%	$11.05	$9.15
9.875%	$10.67	$8.68	10.625%	$11.13	$9.24
10%	$10.75	$8.78	10.75%	$11.21	$9.33
10.125%	$10.82	$8.87	10.875%	$11.29	$9.43

gaged over either a fifteen- or thirty-year period. Borrow $150,000 at 6.5 percent for thirty years, for instance, and you'll pay $948 a month in principal and interest ($150,000 ÷ $1,000 = $150. And $150 × $6.32 = $948).

Types of Mortgages

This is where so many homeowners fall into an unseen trap, partly of their own doing, partly because they are preyed upon by mortgage lenders. Too often the lenders are too eager to push an inappropriate mortgage on a home buyer simply to get the buyer into a particular house, regardless of long-term ramifications. The lender is happy to have pocketed a larger paycheck for closing a larger mortgage; the home buyer is happy to have found a way to afford that dream house.

Both buyer and lender are acting on greedy instincts, and the one potentially hurt the worst is the buyer.

Mortgages are simple products that have been corrupted through the years by bankers and Wall Street types who have designed ever-more-sophisticated mortgages to help more Americans afford a home. Home buyers have been complicit by demanding products that let them buy homes they otherwise couldn't afford.

Two fundamental types of mortgages exist: fixed-rate and adjustable-rate.

The safer of the two is the fixed-rate mortgage. You're locking in an interest rate and, in return, secure a bit of permanency in your family finances because your monthly principal-and-interest payment will never change for as long as you own the house. There is a certain sense of security in that, and a particularly welcome benefit because, over time, your rising income lowers the effective cost of your house. While your monthly mortgage payment might feel constraining in your first few years, as your income rises, a mortgage payment that remains constant will consume a smaller piece of your paycheck.

Fixed-rate mortgages are also simple to understand. They work on those three numbers I previously mentioned—principal, interest rate, and duration. Once you agree to those terms with a lender, and once you sign the paperwork, the numbers are set in stone. You will owe in year 30 the same monthly payment you owed in year 1. Planning for the future is easier because one of the biggest components of your budget won't vary from one year to the next.

Adjustable-rate mortgages add a fourth, fifth, sixth, seventh, and eighth number to the equation: the adjustment period, the amount by which the interest rate can adjust over time, the amount it can adjust each time the mortgage resets, how often it is allowed to reset, and the index rate the mortgage is tied to. That makes these mortgages substantially more complicated, opaque, and risky for the average homeowner. What you pay each month in the early years will likely not be what you pay in later years. Long-range financial planning becomes increasingly challenging because you don't know how your monthly payment might change. And where fixed-rate mortgages grow increasingly less burdensome as your income rises, these so-called ARMs can outpace your income growth, leaving you in a situation where your mortgage consumes a larger portion of your paycheck.

Indeed, ARMs are the very product that created the mess in 2008 that undermined housing prices and brought down banks and mortgage lenders. They are, like Eve's fruit, a danger hidden in plain sight, appealing to those who are lured by the immediacy of the moment and do not think through the impact of their actions.

ARMs charge an initial interest rate that is generally set below prevailing fixed-income rates. That's what makes them so appealing in the moment, because the lower rates lower the monthly cost of your Dream House, at least in the early years, when that initial interest rate is in force. Yet problems lurk in the offing.

When the adjustment period ends, when that initial interest rate begins to reset, your monthly payments can escalate with possibly painful consequences. The adjustment period can stretch from one month to ten years, though most ARMs congregate in the three- to seven-year range. When the resets happen, your interest rate can adjust monthly, semiannually, or yearly, depending on how your contract is written. Rates can adjust up or down depending upon the movement of underlying interest rates in the broader national economy. If interest rates start falling nationally, great; you're ahead of the game because your mortgage suddenly costs less each month. But if rates march higher—or, worse, spike markedly higher in a short period, as they do on occasion—you're potentially in trouble because the increased cost of your mortgage might reach such a level that your paycheck can no longer accommodate your house payment.

How much your rates might change, and how frequently, is spelled out in the mortgage document. If you are ever inclined to pursue an ARM, or are ever pushed toward one by a banker trying to shoehorn you into an expensive house, you must pay attention to the reset frequency and the interest-rate caps. Those rate caps apply to the monthly, semiannual, or annual rate increase the lender can apply to your mortgage, as well as the maximum increase that can occur over the life of the mortgage.

ARMs will differ from one lender to the next, one mortgage to the next, but an example might look like this: The initial interest rate is set at 4 percent when prevailing rates are 5.625 percent on a fixed-rate mortgage. The adjustment period is set at five years, but after that time the rate can adjust every six months, one percentage point at a time, no more than 2 percent in a given year. And over the life of the mortgage, the rate can never be more than 11 percent. On a $200,000 mortgage, that effectively means a doubling of your monthly note, from $955 to, potentially, $1,737 if the lifetime cap is reached in the shortest time.

Can your pocketbook swallow such a dramatic change? Can you live with that risk overhanging your mortgage, overhanging your house? If the answer is no, then you have no reason to buy into the hollow promise that an adjustable-rate mortgage makes homeownership more affordable.

Given the risks, why would anyone want an ARM? They can have their savvy uses, but you must be certain about one or two facts before you agree to such a mortgage.

Home buyers who are confident interest rates are falling might do well in an ARM, because as rates slide lower, their house payment will drop. Moreover, falling rates likely would mean that fixed-rate mortgages will be cheaper in the future than they are today, giving a home buyer the opportunity to refinance into a lower-cost, fixed-rate mortgage before the adjustment period ends on the ARM.

Or you must be certain that you will live in a particular house for a set number of years. In that case, the ARM's initial interest rate, because it is lower than the fixed rate, means a cheaper mortgage payment for the years you're in the house.

The risk, of course, with either of these strategies is that you can't know the answers for sure. You think interest rates are falling, and all the economic pundits in the media are saying that, but some unforeseen shock to the system lurches up to undermine your expectations, and rates surge higher. Your payment surges, too.

Or you expect to move in five years, but unexpected events change your plans, and as the adjustment period on your ARM comes to an end, interest rates are sharply higher than they were when you originally signed for the loan. Again, your payment increases, possibly sharply.

ARMs certainly have their place. But for the majority of American homeowners, a fixed-rate mortgage is the adult equivalent of a child's security blanket. You will always feel comfortable wrapped up in it.

Toxic Waste

As bad as an ARM can be, its cousin, the Option ARM, can be downright toxic to your wealth. Avoid these. They might well be the single worst mortgage product the lending world has ever created.

What was originally designed in the early 1980s as a tool for wealthy borrowers became by the late 1990s a means for the masses to afford too much house without understanding the inherent risks.

Option ARMs offer the *option* to pay one of several different payments each month, including an interest-only mortgage payment that strips out the principal you otherwise should be paying, or a "minimum" payment that's even smaller.

Such payment strategies mean you're not paying down the principal balance on your home. You're only paying interest—and with the minimum payment you're not even paying that. That guarantees a rising mortgage payment in later years. In fact, with the minimum payment option, your principal balance actually grows larger each month because you're not making a full mortgage payment, a characteristic with the distasteful name "negative amortization." Homeowners rarely understand this aspect of Option ARMs. What they do understand, though, are catchy advertising slogans like "Pick-a-Payment Home Loans" and ridiculously low teaser rates of just 1 percent (often good for the first month only!) that lenders use to hawk these toxic mortgages to unsuspecting working-class home buyers.

Sure, Option ARMs allow you to pay a fully amortizing monthly payment, but here's where these mortgages lead buyers astray: The fully amortizing payment for your Dream House is almost always too expensive because the house is too expensive to begin with. But, no worries, the interest-only payment, or, better yet, the minimum payment shaves hundreds, sometimes even $1,000 a month off the mortgage. Suddenly that house that is otherwise way beyond your means is miraculously affordable. So appealing is that result that Countrywide Financial, a mortgage lender that imploded during the housing meltdown, completed $93 billion worth of Option ARMs in 2005, during the height of the lending orgy. At one point, 40 percent of all mortgages in Salinas, California, were Option ARMs, as were 26 percent of mortgages in tony Naples, Florida, and 51 percent of mortgages in all of West Virginia.

But the seeds of disaster were evident. UBS, a Wall Street investment-banking firm, found in a 2007 study that 80 percent of Option ARMs borrowers were only making the minimum payment. Thus, billions of dollars in unpaid principal and interest have accumulated, and that bill is coming due.

The disaster? Well, Option ARMs generally recast themselves after five years, a point at which principal payments become necessary. When that happens, monthly payments can double or triple, effectively making your house unaffordable, leading to foreclosure if you can't sell and get out from under the offending mortgage.

(Continued)

Do not be tempted. A low mortgage payment that seems to help you buy a house you can't afford with a fixed-rate mortgage isn't a miracle. It's a devil in disguise that can ruin your finances and pull your family home right out from under you one day.

The Art of Buying a House

Too many home buyers approach home buying like this: Find a house you love, then hope you can make the finances work with your wallet and the lender. That's backward. At best it's an approach that begets either frustration or heartbreak when you must walk away from the house you really want. Or it causes you to make a rash decision—to buy the house, damn the consequences—that returns one day to haunt your personal finances.

Savvy home buyers reverse that process.

They first tally the sum of cash they can amass from personal savings and by liquidating some or all of their investments—though not retirement-account assets, and I'll explain why in a later chapter. They determine how much money, if any, family might gift or loan to them at favorable rates. Then, off they go to a few lenders to, first, determine how much money they're eligible to borrow based on their income and credit history, and, second, obtain a preapproval letter from a lender. From there, calculating how much house they can truly afford is easy.

Shopping for Interest Rates

When you're looking for a mortgage you are effectively shopping for interest rates. You're searching out the lowest rate with the lowest fees. That will keep the most money in your pocket and over time can amount to savings of tens of thousands of dollars. In that context, comparison shopping for a mortgage just as you would for a new car or a new appliance is crucial to your wealth.

Mortgages are commodities and lenders compete fiercely for business, so you will often find meaningful differences in the rates, fees, and costs associated with a mortgage. Online you will find services like Bankrate.com that aggregate in one place the rates that Internet-based and local lenders in your market are charging for whatever type of mortgage you're seeking, either fixed-rate or adjustable-rate. But Bankrate's local listings aren't necessarily complete, so spend time shopping the banks, savings and loans, and credit unions in your town.

As part of your house-hunting preparations, consider obtaining from your lender that preapproval letter I mentioned a few paragraphs back.

Preapproval letters effectively announce to a seller that you are a serious buyer because you've gone through the process of being preapproved by a mortgage bank. In that process, a lender picks apart your finances, verifies your income, analyzes your credit score, and basically drafts a formal letter stating that you will be allowed to borrow up to a certain dollar amount. Sellers like preapproval letters—and are more willing to negotiate with buyers who have one—because they remove a certain amount of risk. Buyers without preapproved financing might love a house, and might make an offer the seller accepts, but then when the buyer seeks financing the bank says no—and the transaction fails, leaving the seller to start all over again, often having wasted weeks waiting for the process to culminate in that no.

A prequalified letter is a far more informal document in which a lender offers its best guess that you will *probably* be approved for a mortgage up to a certain dollar amount, but there's no guarantee. Sellers are less impressed, because the transaction could still fall apart if your finances don't ultimately meet the bank's standards once the real approval process begins.

That's the smart way to shop for a house. You enter the house-hunting process already confident of your ability to obtain the necessary financing, and you know exactly what price range to shop in. If you can muster, say, $40,000 in cash, and a lender says you're eligible for a mortgage of up to $175,000, you clearly know that your top end is a house priced no higher than $215,000. Knowing this going in will reduce anxiety and temper any potential frustration you might feel at not being able to afford some particular house that you shouldn't have been considering anyway.

Bear in mind, of course, that you don't have to borrow as much money as a lender is willing to offer. Your finances will be better off if you don't. Particularly in so-called easy money periods, lenders are loose with their standards and are often willing to lend more money than is prudent simply for the sake of putting to work all the cash they have available. The downside for you is that you end up in a pricier home that could become a noose around your neck in a family financial crisis, when that bigger mortgage payment torments you every month. And as I hope the previous section on mortgages adequately conveyed, that noose can be exceedingly tight if you're in a too-expensive home by dint of a trendy mortgage.

Better to live more frugally, buying below your means, and in turn saving that extra bit of cash each month that would instead go to the lender. Such a policy will help you build a cash cushion to prepare for rough periods, or to save more for retirement, or to stash away more dollars for your child's future educational costs.

13

Should I Prepay My Mortgage?

People often talk of "investing" in a house. They speak of their home as their biggest investment, and they use the concept of investing as one of their rationales for buying a home in the first place.

Funny, then, that so many don't see paying off their mortgage early as one of the best investments they can make once they own the house.

Prepaying your mortgage represents one of the very few guaranteed rates of return you will find anywhere. With every dollar you include in your monthly mortgage payment beyond the required amount, you are getting a return equal to whatever interest rate your mortgage carries. Homeowners often don't see it this way because the returns don't accumulate on the bottom line as they do with, say, a savings account, where you can see that this month you have more money in your account than you did last month thanks to the interest payment.

Prepaying a mortgage works a bit in reverse. You don't see the interest payments accumulate; you see your principal balance shrink. And when your principal balance is shrinking, the interest you're paying grows increasingly smaller.

Mortgages work by applying the stated interest rate to the remaining principal balance each month. If you have a principal balance of $100,000 on your mortgage in a given month, one-twelfth of the annual interest rate is applied to that balance. A portion of that payment covers the interest due, while the rest reduces the principal so that next month, the interest rate is applied to a slightly lower principal balance. On a $100,000, thirty-year mortgage fixed at 6 percent, it looks like this mathematically:

Month	Beginning Balance	Payment	Principal	Interest	Ending Balance
1	$100,000.00	$599.55	$99.55	$500.00	$99,900.45
2	$99,900.45	$599.55	$100.05	$499.50	$99,800.40
3	$99,800.40	$599.55	$100.55	$499.00	$99,699.85
4	$99,699.85	$599.55	$101.05	$498.50	$99,598.80
5	$99,598.80	$599.55	$101.56	$497.99	$99,497.25

To determine what portion of your payment is principal and what portion is interest, just divide your interest rate by 12, and multiply that result by whatever your principal balance is for any given month. Take a look at Month 3 above. The principal balance that month began at $99,800.40. Multiply that by .005 (6% ÷ 12) and you get $499. That means the remainder of that $599.55 monthly payment goes to paying down your principal.

So imagine what would happen if, in Month 3, you came home with a $10,000 bonus from work and applied the entire amount to paying down a portion of your mortgage in that month:

Month	Beginning Balance	Payment	Principal	Interest	Special Payment	Ending Balance
3	$99,800.40	$599.55	$100.55	$499.00	$10,000	$89,699.85
4	$89,699.85	$599.55	$151.05	$448.50		$89,548.80
5	$89,548.80	$599.55	$151.81	$447.74		$89,396.99

That $10,000 drop in Month 3 means the interest rate is applied to a smaller beginning balance in Month 4. The result:

Even though your monthly payment remains the same at $599.55, the interest you pay in Month 4 is $50 less than it would have been had you not paid down the principal. That $50 is, instead, going to your principal. And that's not just a one-time benefit. Look at Month 5: your interest costs are $50.25 less, that extra quarter coming because of that $50 reduction in Month 4. It's the Miracle of Compounding, which Albert Einstein once called "one of the most powerful forces in the universe."

To bring this example entirely full circle and to show you that paying off your mortgage is an investment, that $50 savings in Month 4 is exactly an annualized 6 percent return on the $10,000 investment you made ($10,000 × .06 = $600, and $600 ÷ 12 = $50). That's the power of prepaying your mortgage, and why it can be so beneficial to your finances. You invested your extra money and received an immediate 6 percent return, the interest rate applied to the mortgage.

Over the long run, the thirty-year duration of your mortgage, extra payments ultimately mean you pay off your debt quicker and you sharply reduce the amount of interest you pay to the lender. In our example, that single, $10,000 payment in Month 3 erases nearly six years' worth of payments and saves a fairly astonishing $38,322.87 in interest payments.

Now, if you are already a homeowner, or when you become one, you will likely receive from your lender a letter offering to help you set up a bimonthly payment plan, in which you will pay your monthly mortgage note every two weeks instead of the single check most homeowners dispatch. That $599.55 monthly payment from our previous example changes to $279.78 every two weeks. No skin off your nose, but the net effect over fifty-two weeks means you're making thirteen full mortgage payments a year instead of twelve—basically adding one more payment every year. That idea of sending your lender an additional payment every year is fantastic. It will trim about five years off that $100,000 mortgage in our example and save roughly $23,600 in interest payments.

But the approach lenders use is bad for your finances.

Agree to their terms and they will charge you several hundred dollars to arrange the account to handle the bimonthly payments. You can accomplish the same end without any cost to you by simply dividing your monthly mortgage payment by 12 and including that sum as additional principal in your monthly mortgage payment.

Keeping with our example, you'd include an additional $49.96 on top of the $599.55 you send to the lender each month. The added benefit is that using this strategy rather than the bank's bimonthly scheme, you're actually saving about $900 more in interest payments over the shortened life of the mortgage.

14

Should I Refinance My Mortgage?

Every time interest rates drop, a refinancing boom ripples across the country as homeowners rush to replace their current mortgages with new mortgages sporting a lower interest rate, thereby lowering their monthly housing cost.

It's a smart way to save money, and an easy way to be a better steward of your financial resources. The savings you achieve by refinancing your mortgage can be used to generate an immediate return on investment by plowing it back into your house in the form of those additional principal payments we just covered, or to help you build added financial security by bulking up your savings, paying down other debts, or preparing for future costs you know are coming.

But don't rush to refinance just because your friends and neighbors are. Refinancing isn't a no-brainer for every homeowner just because rates have drifted lower. There are costs involved in obtaining a new mortgage, and you must take those into account, particularly if you expect to sell your home relatively soon. Moreover, depending on how much time you have remaining before your current mortgage is paid off, refinancing might do you little good, serving only to put thousands of dollars in the lender's pocket.

When to Refi, When to Sit Tight

There's one instance in which refinancing almost always makes sense: If you have an adjustable-rate mortgage and interest rates in the broader economy are headed up, by all means refinance. You will save yourself dollars and, possibly more important, untold angst. When interest rates are going up, even if your ARM's rate remains constant for another year or two, you are taking on big risk. By the time your mortgage begins to reset, rates could be sharply higher, dramatically increasing your monthly payments. Thus, even if refinancing into a fixed-rate mortgage means your rate bumps up above what you're currently paying with the ARM, it's still smarter to pay a little more now than a lot more later.

You will know, by the way, that interest rates are rising in the economy; that information is widely noted in the mainstream media.

Now, the decision to refinance isn't so easy when you're considering trading one fixed-rate mortgage for another. Clearly, you'd contemplate that possibility only if current interest rates are below the rate on your existing mortgage; otherwise it makes no sense financially. But how far below your existing rate do current interest rates need to fall before refinancing makes sense for you? That's the question homeowners struggle with.

As with so much in life, no one-size-fits-all answer exists. What's right for one homeowner might not be right for another.

At issue are the underlying costs and how long it will take to recoup those costs through the savings generated by the new mortgage. Lenders hit you with a variety of charges when you obtain a mortgage. There are sundry fees for notary services, document processing, filing deeds, appraisal and courier services, and such. Some mortgage lenders will charge so-called points, effectively a fee for originating the loan. These points represent a percentage of the mortgage. One point equals one percent, so that one point on a $100,000 mortgage is equivalent to $1,000.

If you pay something like $4,000 in various fees and charges, and you're saving $100 a month with a new mortgage, you're looking at a payback period of forty months, or more than three years.

That's your first consideration when contemplating a refinancing: How many more years do you expect to remain in your house? If you spend $4,000 to save $100 a month, yet you plan to move in a year or two, the outlay for the new mortgage makes no sense. You'd ultimately have more money in your possession if you stuck with your current mortgage.

If you plan to live in your home for many years—particularly if you plan to live there for the duration—then just about any refinancing that lowers your rate will probably make sense, since you'll have so many months to recoup the costs. Still, run through the calculations so that you'll know exactly what the mortgage will cost you and where the break even point is on the calendar. It's a simple calculation:

- Subtract the proposed monthly mortgage payment from your current payment. This is your monthly savings.
- Ask your lender for a so-called HUD statement that tallies all the costs and points you'll pay. If you haven't reached that stage of the mortgage process, ask the lender for a breakdown of the costs you will be expected to pay. Divide those costs by the savings. The result represents the number of months you'll pay before you recoup all your costs. Every payment after that month represents true savings.

Points: Yes or No?

Most homeowners believe that not paying points is good, and that paying points means the lender is effectively shaking you down in a bad way.

This is simply untrue. When you pay points, you are buying

(Continued)

down the interest rate that will apply to your mortgage over its lifespan. If you run through the math, you might find that paying points is a wise move indeed, depending on how long you plan to keep the new mortgage.

,   Consider this example, using real interest rates available in late 2008 on a thirty-year, fixed-rate $200,000 mortgage. One lender offered 6.5 percent for zero points; a competitor advertised 5.625 percent if you paid one point. All other costs equal, that one point means you're paying an additional $2,000 up front just to lock in the lower rate and a monthly payment about $113 cheaper. Many people will look at that and say I don't want to spring for an additional $2,000—often because they've scraped together as much cash as possible for the down payment.

Yet over the life of the loan, that $2,000 expense will save nearly $41,000 in interest. Even if you have to finance the points by rolling the cost into the principal mortgage balance, you're still saving $100 a month on the payment and more than $40,000 over thirty years. (At savings of $100 a month, you'll break even on the points after less than two years in the house.)

My message: Don't stubbornly save a few dollars up front at the cost of many dollars in the end. Paying points is not necessarily bad. You just have to run through the calculations to determine the impact in your particular situation.

Things to Remember When Refinancing

First, refinance into a mortgage that maintains the same number of years you have remaining on your current mortgage. What good does it do you to save $100 a month if you have twenty-five years left on your current mortgage but you refinance for thirty years? You've just added five years of additional payments, and that will exceed what you otherwise would have saved. So if you have twenty-five years still to pay off your house, refinance into a twenty-five-year mortgage. You won't see mortgages necessarily advertised that way, but lenders are not limited to mortgages of fifteen and thirty years; they'll make a mortgage for any number of years.

Second, if you've lived in your home for many years already—usually a dozen or more—refinancing probably won't make sense unless the interest-rate differential is dramatic. After so many years, your monthly payments are really eating into the principal balance. Thus, unless prevailing rates are sharply lower, you won't see much savings by refinancing. Depending on the costs, you might not even recoup your outlay before your mortgage is paid off.

Finally, to the degree you can, avoid so-called cash-out refinancing. This is where borrowers refinance and, as part of the process, pull out a big chunk of the equity they've amassed in their home. This is the disastrous strategy many consumption-addicted homeowners relied on during the housing bubble of the early- and mid-2000s. They looked upon their home as a personal ATM, using any increase in home equity as a reason to refinance so that they could get at the money and use it to buy second homes, pay for vacations and new cars and boats, or invest in the stock market.

They were unwittingly building their own house of cards.

As home prices declined, their house was no longer worth the value of the outstanding mortgage and second mortgage and home-equity line of credit they'd used to tap into their home's equity. Unable to sell and repay the balance due, either they defaulted on their mortgage or the bank was forced to foreclose on the property—and the downward spiral began.

If you absolutely must pull money out of your house, do so for a valid reason, such as a medical emergency. But neither a new car you covet, nor a vacation you think you deserve, nor a spin around Wall Street is a reason to drain the equity in your home.

You will be better served by allowing the money to remain effectively locked up in the bricks and mortar that is your house.

This way you can call on that equity later in life, when you retire and possibly downsize to a smaller house or move to a retirement home. The equity you've built up over decades will be there to fund your life when you need it most.

15

How Do I Work to Prepare for Winter?

Do you want to be the ant or the grasshopper?

So well known is Aesop's fable about those two insects that you will undoubtedly remember that the ant spent the summer laying in assets for the coming lean season, while the grasshopper played. When winter came, RIP, poor grasshopper.

Retirement is the lean season of your life. The time for you to work and gather assets was back in your spring and summer. Once the cold winds begin blowing, your source of sustenance is the money you dutifully stored up during those warmer, working days.

Many options for saving for retirement exist, each packaged with its own set of benefits and caveats. As with investing itself, your retirement is best served by spreading your assets among those various options. This chapter will help you do that by explaining the different options and how they're best employed. I will also spend some time on asset allocation, the strategy of diversifying your investments across multiple types of assets, currencies, countries, and such. Our goal is simple: to help you build over time a portfolio that is flexible, tax-savvy, and diversified so that like Aesop's ant's, your mound is well-stocked for your coming winter.

The options I'm talking about are the variety of retirement-savings accounts in which you can stash money in a tax-advantaged fashion. These include employer-sponsored retirement-savings plans like the ubiquitous 401(k) and others of similar design, several different Individual Retirement Accounts, and a collection of annuities. Each aims to get you to—and through—retirement, but they do so in slightly different ways, and understanding how each operates will help you make wiser decisions on which is best for you.

The 401(k)

With nearly 60 million Americans participating in some 436,000 plans spread across businesses big, small, and huge, there's a very good chance you have some money in a 401(k) account, or any of the similarly named employer-sponsored retirement accounts such as 403(b) and 457. There's also a pretty good chance you could be managing your account much more wisely.

Study after study has shown that too many workers pay too little attention to their 401(k) plan, content to just let the account sit there accumulating a little money now and then, assuming they even contribute to their plan in the first place. Indeed, between 20 percent and 25 percent of all eligible workers don't even participate. Given that the vast majority of employers match some portion of your contribution, failing to enroll in your 401(k) plan is little different from telling your bank to skip the interest payment on some portion of your savings. You're giving away money.

Too often, workers demonstrate an employer bias by loading their account with company stock. You might feel upbeat about your company's prospects, but, then again, so did all those Enron workers left with barren 401(k) accounts after management there destroyed the company.

Many workers are too content to let their employer choose where their money is invested. Though this is changing, often that means workers end up with cash sitting in the most risk-averse investment options in the plan, usually a money-market fund of some sort. Risk-averse might sound comforting, particularly after the stock-market crash of 2008. In reality, risk aversion can leave your account far too anemic to support you in retirement, because your money didn't work as hard as you needed it to during your career.

A 401(k) plan is increasingly one of the most important retirement-savings accounts you can own, given the demise of company-sponsored pensions and, as mentioned earlier in this book, that Social Security is designed to buffer against poverty in old age, not to be the main source of retirement income. How well you ultimately live in retirement depends on your efforts at building some measure of a nest egg while you're working. Start with your 401(k).

At its core, a 401(k) is a tax-deferred investment account. Every dollar you invest in your 401(k) escapes the state and federal taxes that are applied to your paycheck. Your contribution has the effect, then, of reducing your taxable income, but not on a dollar-for-dollar basis. In practical terms, that means that if you're in, say, the 25 percent tax bracket, every dollar you put into a 401(k) costs you only 75 cents. By that I mean that if you contribute $100 to a 401(k) plan every month, your take-home pay is only reduced by $75.

Ultimately, you will pay taxes on this money, when you begin withdrawing it in retirement. At that time, you will pay taxes on the principal you invested as well as on the gains you have accumulated, and you will do so at your ordinary income-tax rate. You won't be allowed to touch your money until you're at least fifty-nine and a half years old.

Take out any money sooner and you pay ordinary income taxes on the entire sum of money you withdraw, plus an additional 10 percent penalty—not to mention that you are robbing yourself of substantially more money later. For instance, if you yank $10,000 out of your 401(k) at age thirty-five and you're in that 25 percent tax bracket, you owe taxes of $2,500 and a penalty of $1,000, for a harsh bite that leaves you a net, spendable amount of just $6,500. Worse, at a fairly conservative 7 percent annual rate of return, that $10,000, over the next thirty-two years (when you reach full retirement age at sixty-seven), would have grown to more than $87,000. Even if you retired early, at fifty-nine and a half, the money you pulled from your 401(k) would have reached nearly $53,000.

Participating in a 401(k)

For many, a 401(k) plan is largely a nuisance, according to studies. Personal finance for a lot of people is on par with dental surgery, and the idea that you are responsible for managing your own account and picking your own investments and trying to figure out how much to invest in what particular option—generally with little help—leaves many workers feeling they've been thrown into the deep end of the pool without swimming lessons.

But 401(k) plans require very little effort beyond signing up and spending a few minutes to make sure your money is invested properly. And that part about "invested properly" isn't as hard or as time consuming as you might think, as I'll show you in a bit. You don't have to babysit the account every week or every month or even every quarter. The only maintenance you should perform is, one, rebalancing your portfolio once a year or so to reduce exposure to the assets that have grown too large, and increasing exposure to the assets that have grown too small and, two, increasing your contribution annually so that you're saving adequately for retirement.

The good news is that these days many companies have autopilot features that do almost all of the hard lifting for you—even the enrollment. With the passage of pension-reform legislation in 2006, a large number of companies altered their 401(k) programs to make them more effective for workers. Companies once relied on employees to proactively sign up, and to proactively pick how they wanted their money invested, and to proactively choose at some point to increase their contributions to the plan. If a worker enrolled and wasn't sure what to do with the money, the company automatically defaulted the cash into a safe, money-market fund. Companies recognized all along that this was a bad strategy, because it stunted the growth of employees' accounts. Nevertheless, in America's overly litigious society, companies were rightly terrified that making any investment decision for a worker might ultimately expose the company to a lawsuit if those investments performed poorly.

Now, with the reform legislation as a shield, companies are free to act in their workers' best interest. That means many companies now automatically enroll employees in the 401(k) plan unless a worker opts out. It means that companies automatically default workers into an appropriate mutual fund, often so-called target-date funds that aim to mature as you near retirement, growing increasingly conservative as you get older. And it means that companies automatically start you saving at 2 percent or 3 percent of your salary and automatically increase that amount by one percentage point each year up to a certain level.

To stop any of this requires that you, the worker, approach your human resources department and specifically seek the paperwork necessary to decline these automatic features. And that's the point: Companies are taking advantage of the Great Inertia that pervades humans. As a group, we humans aren't quick to change what doesn't hurt us. If our employers takes 3 percent of our salary out of every paycheck and we don't really feel the pain, then taking the time to wander down to the HR department and find the person who knows where the right forms are, then taking those forms back to our desk and fill out, only to wander back down to HR to return the forms…that's much more of a personal annoyance than dealing with the absence of 3 percent of our paycheck.

That your company is making decisions for you doesn't mean you ignore your 401(k) plan until you retire. If nothing else, you need to be aware of where your money is invested in case it's not appropriate for your needs or risk tolerance.

Managing Your 401(k)

So here's what you need to know about managing your 401(k). And I promise, none of this is complicated or time consuming, but it can help you build a meaningful balance over time, and that will make your retirement all the easier.

Accept some risk. The younger you are, the more risk you are able to withstand, because you still have many years to work. That means you can recoup the losses that might occur when the market turns down, as it does from time to time. Though the stock-market crash of 2008 was dreadfully painful to watch, the losses that occurred in 401(k) plans will likely be erased by the time twenty- and thirty- and forty-something workers get around to retiring in three or four decades or more. When stock prices are low, that allows you to buy more shares for the same number of dollars, and as the market goes higher over the years, those shares will benefit your account greatly.

Even workers in their fifties will likely recoup much of what they lost, although once you're in your fifties and into your early sixties, you should be moving increasingly into bonds and some cash as a way to cushion against stock-market risk. Even after you're retired, you'll want some exposure to stocks, since, statistically, you are likely to live another sixteen to twenty years, and could well live much longer than that. Indeed, centenarians—those people who celebrate their hundredth birthday—represent one of the fastest-growing demographic groups in America. Therefore, you'll want some amount of stocks in your nest egg to help the portfolio keep pace with inflation.

So don't avoid risk in your 401(k). Risk is a counterpart of return. If you put all your money in riskless investments, your money has no chance of growing into a sum large enough to meet your needs in retirement.

Stick to index funds. The 401(k) plans are notorious for offering ho-hum investment options. Part of the reason is that the 401(k) industry typically limits plan offerings to just a handful of funds, because studies have shown time and again that more than that causes confusion among employees, who will often give up on investing in the plan because of the stress of having to choose among all the different funds. Part of the reason is the fund industry, where most managers fail to do as well as the S&P 500 or whatever index they benchmark themselves against—and those who do beat the index generally can't keep it up for very long.

So, there's no reason to stress yourself out trying to choose between funds, and there's no reason to risk underperformance in your account. An index fund addresses both issues by narrowing your choices to one fund and by insuring that your investments will perform in line with the index. Moreover, you'll pay smaller fees, since index funds, as I mentioned earlier, are usually cheaper than actively managed funds.

The problem you might run into, however, is that, aside from an S&P 500 fund and a bond index fund, most 401(k) plans will not be loaded with a wide selection of index funds. If yours is one that isn't, there's not much you can do, but that's okay. Structure the meat of your portfolio around the S&P and bond index funds, and then pick the best actively managed small-cap, mid-cap, and international fund you have on your list. The two index funds will do much of the heavy lifting, and the actively managed funds will work to sweeten the returns a bit.

Some 401(k) plans sneak in a very good fund manager from time to time, and if you have access to one of those, take advantage of it, if you want to. Just remember, though, that fund managers change jobs, and those really good returns can tail off if the manager leaves. So occasionally you'll have to pay attention to who's running the ship. Other plans provide a so-called brokerage window that allows you access to just about any stock, bond, or mutual fund on Wall Street. If your plan offers this, then you have an opportunity to own the best index funds available. That will take some research on your part (see the mutual fund chapter), but it will serve you well in the end.

Increase contributions: Every year, aim to increase the amount of money you're stashing away in your 401(k) account. Your ultimate goal over time is to contribute each year as much money as the Internal Revenue Service allows. In 2009, that limit is $16,500. If you're over fifty-five, the IRS also allows for an additional $5,500 as part of a "catch-up" provision so that you can build a bigger nest egg more rapidly.

Unless you are a highly compensated worker, you're probably thinking there's no way you can afford to pull between $16,500 and $22,000 out of your paycheck every year. You don't have to. Start by contributing what you can afford. If that's just 1 percent of your paycheck, then that's better than nothing and it starts you moving toward retirement wealth. My advice is that you try to contribute at least up to the amount of your company's matching contribution. So, for instance, if your company matches fifty cents for every dollar you contribute up to 3 percent of your pay, then try to start your contributions at 3 percent of pay so that you capture every bit of free money your company is willing to give you.

Periodically, after you've begun contributing, raise your contribution rate. You can do this whenever you want to during the year, but I would encourage you to consider doing it semiannually or, at the very least, annually. At whatever interval you choose, increase your contributions by one percentage point—more if you can afford it. A painless way to fit the increase into your budget is through whatever raises you earn. Split your raise so that some portion of it goes to your 401(k) plan while the rest stays in your paycheck. With this strategy, you are increasing your wealth without affecting your current lifestyle, and you're allowing yourself a little more money to modestly improve your standard of living.

Rebalance. Asset prices move up and down and around every day. Over time, the amount of stocks you own relative to bonds, or the amount of foreign stocks you own relative to U.S. stocks, will grow too small or too large. You want to fix that, because when those balances are out of whack you take on greater risk.

In the late 1990s, amid the technology and Internet euphoria, investors who owned tech-heavy mutual funds discovered a painful reality when share prices cracked: They had greedily or absent-mindedly allowed their stock funds to grow large, and when shares prices fell sharply, their big profits turned into big losses. One of Wall Street's favorite aphorisms fits here: Pigs get fat; hogs get slaughtered. The point is that tech investors could have avoided the fate of hogs if they'd simply been happy to fatten up on technology and then move on. Instead, they grew fat and then continued feeding at the trough, trying to eat up more and more gains. If they'd sold out with big profits and gone looking for stocks in undervalued sectors to own—and there were many at the time—they would have largely missed the devastation that pushed tech-stock prices down 75 percent to 99 percent in many cases.

This same principle applies to 401(k) plans. During bull markets for stocks, share prices can surge in relation to bonds and other assets, and you can end up in a situation in which 90 percent of your portfolio is in stocks when you originally wanted just 80 percent. That means the bond and cash component of your account has shriveled to 10 percent from your original target of 20 percent. To remedy this, you should rebalance your portfolio on occasion, usually once a year.

Rebalancing is nothing more complicated than selling that portion of the fund that has grown too large and using those proceeds to buy more of the asset that has become too small in your account. In the example above, you'd sell enough of your stock mutual fund to bring it down to 80 percent of your account's overall value, and you would distribute that money across bonds and cash to bring them back up to their appropriate levels. In effect, rebalancing simply means you're selling high-priced assets, or those that have had a strong run, to buy low-priced assets, or those that have lagged in price. In doing so, you are adhering to what might be Wall Street's two most famous aphorisms: "Buy low, sell high" and "No one ever goes broke taking a profit."

Don't rebalance too frequently, though. You want to let your winners ride for a while and you don't want to rack up a bunch of trading costs, since that eats into your returns. The ultimate goal isn't to sell high-priced assets at their peak, or to buy low-priced assets at their absolute nadir. It's simply to take profits on occasion and to reinvest that money in assets that are still relatively inexpensive, because the high-priced assets will inevitably fall in value and the underpriced assets will inevitably rise in value, and rebalancing is a way for you to avoid the former while benefiting from the latter.

Leave your money alone. Finally, do not take your money out of your 401(k) plan when you change jobs, and do not borrow against your 401(k).

Studies by Fidelity Investments, the big Boston-based mutual fund company, and others regularly show that workers who leave one job for another will all too frequently cash out their 401(k) balance at the old employer and spend the money. Studies also show that roughly one-fifth of workers had borrowed money from their 401(k) account as of 2008.

Neither is a particularly good idea.

When you change jobs and decide to empty your account, you unnecessarily impose on yourself taxes and penalties for raiding the account before age fifty-nine and a half. Depending on your tax bracket, that can reduce your account value by 30 percent or 40 percent or more. Not only that, because you're spending a retirement asset that would otherwise have grown through the years, you are forsaking a substantially larger sum of money years into the future, when you're retired and looking for all the income you can muster to pay for housing and food and medical bills and electricity and such.

Instead of raiding your account when you leave a job, you have three other options that are much wiser. Let the money stay where it is and continue to grow. Transfer the money into your new employer's 401(k) plan, assuming your new employer allows that. Or roll the money into an IRA (more on those in the next chapter). Any of these three options avoids taxes and penalties and gives your money many more years to grow in value so that it can support you in retirement.

As for borrowing from your 401(k) plan, people will often make the argument that you are borrowing from yourself and, thus, repaying yourself with interest and, therefore, a 401(k) loan is the best source of borrowing since you're not repaying a bank. There is some logic to that, and a small loan could be viewed as the fixed-income portion of your account, replacing the bond or cash component, since the loan generates a rate of return in line with current interest rates. But there are also substantial caveats and risks you must be aware of before taking out a 401(k) loan.

First, you're not really borrowing money from yourself. You are selling off assets in your account and taking a partial withdrawal, and so long as you repay the money the IRS doesn't imposes taxes and fees. Nevertheless, the loan means that the money that was once at work for you in stocks and bonds is no longer at work; it's earning whatever interest rate your company charges for a 401(k) loan, usually one or two percentage points above the prime rate (you can find that at Bankrate.com, under the "Compare Rates" tab).

Loan repayment, meanwhile, is made with after-tax dollars, not pretax dollars, so the impact on your paycheck is larger than the contribution itself. Moreover, that money will be taxed again when you finally withdraw it in retirement, so you're paying taxes twice on the same dollars.

Perhaps the worst side effect stems from a job loss or your decision to change jobs. Companies generally require workers repay an outstanding 401(k) loan balance within thirty to sixty days of leaving their job. If you can't come up with a large enough lump sum to cover the balance, the IRS considers that sum a partial withdrawal and you will owe taxes and penalties.

All in all, borrowing from your 401(k) is generally not a strategy you should pursue. The money is there for one purpose and that's retirement. It's not a savings account to draw on for consumer whims.

Companies regularly offer a wide range of educational material, sometimes even person-to-person or telephone-based help in properly structuring the investments in a 401(k) plan. Your company wants to see you succeed. But if you're uncertain of what funds you should be picking in your plan, or you just want the comfort of having a professional guide you, then invest a little money and time in a fee-only financial planner who works on an hourly basis. These planners aren't in the business of trying to sell you on any particular product. They're proving a service for a fee, that service being the research and advice necessary to put you into the types of investments that best fit your needs. To find fee-only planners where you live, check out the websites for the Financial Planning Association (www.fpanet.org) or the National Association of Personal Financial Advisors (www.napfa.org).

Company Stock: Too Much of a Potentially Bad Thing

Enron isn't the only poster child for financial catastrophe, and disaster doesn't arrive solely in the form of corrupt company management. Sometimes it comes in the form of unforeseen market events that destroy an otherwise good company.

When the housing bubble burst and undermined the banking and brokerage sector, publicly traded banks such as Indymac and Washington Mutual failed, as did investment-banking legend Lehman Brothers. Their shares were valueless. Quasifederal but publicly traded housing agency Fannie Mae was forced into the arms of the government and its stock plunged to just pennies a share from nearly sixty-five dollars in a little more than a year. Brokerage firms Merrill Lynch and Morgan Stanley dived in value, Morgan at one point slumping to just over six dollars a share from highs once north of seventy dollars.

In each crash, employees who had invested their 401(k) contributions in company stock suffered mightily as the size of their nest egg shriveled with every passing day and every tick lower of the company's stock price.

This destruction of retirement wealth is avoidable. Limit the amount of stock you own in your company, no matter how good or how strong you think your company is, and no matter how many decades it has managed good economies and bad. Lehman Brothers, after all, was more than 150 years old, and had survived every major event in U.S. history from the Civil War to the Great Depression to world wars and major recessions and horrendous government policies. And then came the greatest accumulation of societal debt in history, punctuated by overleveraged homeowners and complex mortgage-related investment products that unexpectedly brought down one of the most famous names on Wall Street and, in the process, wiped away an estimated $10 billion in employee retirement savings.

In the span of less than a decade, then, you have multiple examples demonstrating the risk you bear in keeping too much company stock in your retirement account.

At most, limit your ownership of company stock to 10 percent of the value of your account, and preferably less than that.

(Continued)

If your company's stock outperforms the market as a whole and you realize one day that company stock represents 15 percent or 20 percent or more of your account value, sell off enough shares to bring that percentage back in line. If your company pays its contribution to your account in company stock, keep a small portion if you wish, but sell off the bulk of it as soon as you can and use that money to diversify into other holdings, preferably holdings unrelated to your industry. As a Lehman employee, for instance, ownership of stock in a bunch of banks and brokerage firms, even if you were really familiar with them, would still have generated much pain in your account during the 2008 crash. Better to move into other industries to balance out the risk.

Think about it this way: Your financial life is already tied to your employer by way of your paycheck, so lashing your retirement to the same wagon is double jeopardy. If your company fails, you not only lose your source of income, you lose all or a great portion of your future income, too. You might not have enough years left in the workforce to replace that loss.

16

What Can Make Old Age More Secure for Me?

The Individual Retirement Account (IRA) is a relatively simple creature, a basic tax-deferred retirement account. But whether or not you're eligible for that tax-advantaged saving is one of the more complex calculations in personal finance.

At a basic level, the IRA functions much like a 401(k) plan in that your money grows without being taxed until you retire, at which point the original contributions and all the profits are taxed at ordinary income rates. Moreover, you can't touch the money until you are fifty-nine and a half, or else you're paying those taxes and penalties again. Beyond that there are substantive differences.

Foremost is the fact that IRA contributions don't come through payroll deduction, as they do with a 401(k). The money you invest is after-tax dollars. But you get to deduct all or a portion of the contribution on your income-tax return.

Complex

This, though, is where numbing complexity sets in. Your ability to deduct your contribution each year—and how much you can deduct—depends on a wide range of factors such as age, income, marital status, participation in an employer-sponsored retirement plan, whether you're self-employed, and whether you and a spouse file joint or individual tax returns. Depending on how those factors interact, you may be eligible for a full or partial deduction or for no deduction at all. IRS Publication 590, which you can find online at IRS.gov (search Publication 590), spells out all the various eligibility guidelines and how they interact.

Assuming you can claim the largest deduction, in 2008 that would have limited you to $5,000, plus a $1,000 catch-up provision for savers over fifty-five years old. Starting in 2009, the limit is indexed to inflation, in $500 increments, meaning you can contribute $5,000 plus a potential amount for inflation, but only when the cumulative impact of inflation necessitates a $500 increase. Because the contribution level is so much smaller, and because no one is matching your IRA contribution, you should first fund a 401(k) if you have one, and then stick any extra dollars you can muster into an IRA, assuming you are eligible for the deduction.

Diverse Holdings

IRAs, however, outshine 401(k) plans when it comes to breadth. Inside an IRA you can own a much wider array of assets than is available in a typical 401(k). Depending on which financial firm you use, your IRA can hold everything from basic stocks and bonds and mutual funds to certificates of deposit, futures and options contracts, gold and silver coins, even real estate, such as rental properties.

That you can own a wide variety doesn't mean, of course, that you should. That's particularly true with real estate. You can make a good case for owning gold in an IRA, since it serves as an insurance policy against runaway inflation. And, assuming you know what you're doing, options can be a relatively safe way to protect your portfolio against a market correction or to generate additional income with certain strategies. But real estate can be really troublesome inside an IRA, despite the rhetoric you will occasionally hear from IRA providers that focus exclusively on alternative assets like real estate.

The key here is this: IRAs allow you to contribute only a relatively small sum every year, assuming you're eligible. Now, let's go from there...assume you own a rental property inside your IRA. Clearly, you'll have insurance on the property to cover it against a catastrophe. In this case, let's assume your rental property is in Florida, along the Gulf Coast, where policies often stipulate a 2 percent or 5 percent deductible, meaning you're responsible for the first 2 percent to 5 percent of damage caused by a storm. And then along comes a Katrina or an Andrew or a Gustav and destroys your $400,000 rental home, and your policy stipulates you're responsible for the first 4 percent. What happens if you don't have the necessary $20,000 in your IRA? If you're only eligible to deduct $6,000 in this particular year, how do you repair the damage so that the place is habitable and able to generate rental income again? IRS laws forbid you to fund those costs with outside dollars. Every dollar must come from inside the IRA itself. In short, you have a tremendous headache on your hands.

Therefore, real estate is generally not the best option for an IRA unless the account is seriously fat with cash and you have a big enough cushion to cover a large, unexpected event.

Traditional and Rollover IRAs

Though you will sometimes hear the terms "traditional IRA" and "rollover IRA," the two are identical. A traditional IRA is one you open and fund with after-tax dollars, up to your annual contribution limit. A rollover is the same IRA, just one in which you fund the account with money from another IRA or from your employer's 401(k) plan. In the case of a rollover, you're allowed to roll the entire balance of another retirement account into your IRA, even if that balance far exceeds the IRA's annual contribution limit. This rollover strategy is the path you should pursue when you leave a job and can't—or don't want to—leave behind your 401(k) balance, or a new employer won't allow you to transfer into its 401(k) plan your assets from a previous job. Directing those dollars into a rollover won't expose you to the temptation of spending your retirement fund prematurely and, in the process, losing a large piece of it to taxes and penalties. Brokerage firms and banks offer IRAs, and to simplify the process they will fill out the paperwork necessary for transferring your assets.

If your eligibility allows you to fund an IRA alongside your 401(k), consider using the IRA as a complement to the investment options inside your 401(k). A portfolio isn't a bunch of separate accounts you manage independent of one another; it's a unified whole in which all the various components work together. Where 401(k) plans are deficient in the options they offer, IRAs provide access to nearly the whole universe of useful investments. And where IRAs limit your contributions, 401(k) plans let you save larger sums.

Consider using the 401(k) as the core of your retirement savings, owning there the S&P 500 and bond index funds. There's a good reason for that: 401(k) plans are institutionally priced and you'll often find the index funds are cheaper in a 401(k) than in a retail account like an IRA or a standard brokerage account. That will help keep your costs as low as possible. Then, use the IRA as your satellite account, the account through which you buy the complementary investments like the small and midsized company funds, the international funds, maybe even a gold fund or a small bit of gold bullion as insurance against economic instability or inflation.

As noted earlier, most 401(k) plans probably won't have a broad selection of stellar funds beyond an S&P index fund. But in an IRA you'll be able to buy just about any fund you want, so you can round out your portfolio with standout index funds and

ETFs, or even the actively managed funds that are clearly long-term superstars.

Two final facts to know about IRAs: First, you cannot borrow against the value as you can in a 401(k). Second, the government requires you to begin drawing down the account balance by April 1 of the year after you hit seventy and a half. This is what's known as a "required distribution," and you cannot avoid it, even if you don't need the money. Fail to take the distribution when mandated and the IRS will fine you 50 percent of the amount of money you should have otherwise withdrawn.

If you really don't need the money, then draw it out, pay the taxes due, and then stick that cash in a Roth IRA, where it will grow tax-free for the rest of your life, but more on that strategy in the next section on Roth accounts.

Self-Employment Income

One of the eligibility hurdles that will keep you from contributing to an IRA is income. If you earn more than a certain amount of money—more than $105,000 as an individual in 2009, or $169,000 as a couple—you cannot deduct contributions to an IRA.

There is, though, potentially another avenue, the SEP IRA. Many workers these days moonlight as freelancers, as consultants, or as home-based entrepreneurs hawking goods and services directly or over the Internet. If you report self-employment income on your tax returns, you can contribute to a SEP. The greatest benefit of a SEP is that you can save substantially more money than with a traditional IRA, as much as 20 percent of your net self-employment income, and contribute that to a SEP IRA, up to $49,000.

Though the initials stand for Simplified Employee Pension,

(Continued)

SEPs operate just like IRAs, giving you wide berth in terms of investment options. SEPs are typically available from the same financial-services firms that provide IRAs.

Nondeductible IRA

To add another layer of complexity, you could contribute to a nondeductible IRA, which allows you to save in a tax-deferred manner, but doesn't allow you to write off the contribution on your tax returns each year. The benefit to these IRAs is that because you're not claiming a tax deduction on the way in, you can withdraw your contribution tax-free and without penalty any time you want, even before age fifty-nine and a half. You will pay taxes on any gains, though, and penalties if you pull out those gains before retirement.

But don't go lightly into a nondeductible IRA. There are some serious considerations that, if you ignore them, can cause you financial pain. The IRS requires that you file Form 8606 with your tax returns, noting the existence of a nondeductible IRA. Forget to do that and you owe the government fifty dollars plus interest for every year you owned the account but didn't file the necessary paperwork. Worse is the fact that if you can't show the IRS that you filed Form 8606, the government assumes that your withdrawal came from a deductible IRA and, thus, your contributions are taxed, meaning you will have paid taxes on the same dollars twice.

For most savers, a nondeductible IRA is the IRA of last resort, useful only when you've maxed out other tax-advantaged options and you still have additional cash you want to save for retirement. If that's the case for you, then just make sure you don't commingle money in a deductible and a nondeductible IRA. The paperwork will be easier on you if you keep the accounts at separate firms and you remember to file Form 8606 every year.

The Roth IRA and 401(k)

For all their benefits, one of the bigger knocks against the IRA and the 401(k) is the tax bite. As I noted, the distributions you ultimately withdraw in retirement from either account are taxed as ordinary income, which tends to be the highest rates in the federal tax code, though that could certainly change from time to time under changing presidential and congressional leadership.

The Roth IRA and 401(k) plans address this to a degree, and can be savvier options for some workers, particularly younger workers.

Roth contributions come from after-tax dollars, meaning your money goes to work in a Roth only after you've paid your taxes. So, your contribution to a Roth is actually smaller than it is with a traditional IRA, where every dollar you invest goes to work without the burden of taxation. Your benefit comes on the backside, though. Roth investments grow tax-free, as in the other retirement programs, but when you withdraw the dollars later in life, they come out tax-free. This makes a Roth one of the sweetest options for retirement planning.

In a purely mathematical sense, a Roth IRA or 401(k) and a regular IRA or 401(k) would yield the same end result in a static world. By that I mean if you're in, say, the 28 percent tax bracket and invest $100 each in a traditional IRA and a Roth IRA at the same moment, and they each earn identical returns over an identical number of years, the final value of the two accounts will mirror each other. That's because, with the Roth, you're putting after-tax dollars to work, meaning fewer dollars, but they're never taxed again. The traditional IRA puts more dollars to work initially, but taxes all of them on the way out. Here's how it looks:

	Roth	Traditional
Contribution	$100.00	$100.00
Tax Rate (going in)	28%	0%
Net Contribution	$72.00	$100.00
Annual Return	8%	8%
Years Invested	25	25
Gross return	$493.09	$684.85
Tax Rate (coming out)	0%	28%
Net return	$493.09	$493.09

But here's where reality intervenes. The tax world is not static. It's progressive. The more income you earn, the higher your ordinary income-tax rates. And that's where Roth accounts shine, and why they make so much sense for younger workers with a couple decades or more to go before retiring.

Workers generally start their careers in the lowest tax brackets and progressively work their way higher through the years. If you begin saving early and in a relatively low tax bracket, you have a very good chance of ending up in a much higher tax bracket in retirement simply because of the nest egg you accumulated and the income it ultimately generates for you one day. If you save in a traditional IRA, you skip tax payments in the early years only to pay taxes at much higher rates in retirement. A Roth reverses that process. You'll pay taxes on the money before you invest it, but at rates of between 15 percent and 25 percent, the range most workers fall into in 2009. Yet you will skip taxes altogether in retirement, when your income could push you into tax brackets of 33 percent to 35 percent, possibly higher depending upon the actions of future presidential administrations.

Younger workers aren't the only ones who might benefit from a Roth. For older workers with substantial assets already saved in a traditional 401(k) or IRA, a Roth offers tax-free access to a portion of your account, allowing you to better manage your tax situation by drawing down tax-free dollars, whereas if the income came from a taxable retirement account it could push you into a higher tax bracket.

Older parents and grandparents could benefit from a Roth IRA in college planning for kids and grandchildren. So long as the Roth IRA is at least five years old, and you are at least fifty-nine and a half, you can pull the money out tax-free to pay for educational costs. Because federal financial-aid formulas don't take retirement assets into account, the money in your Roth won't affect the calculus that helps determine a student's eligibility for financial aid, if that's necessary.

Moreover, a Roth IRA can be a great tool for transferring assets to heirs. Where traditional IRAs impose a minimum distribution requirement at age seventy and a half, Roths don't, one of their additional advantages. You can keep your money in the account and never be required to pull out a penny. As such, you could invest in a Roth IRA through the years, or roll the assets of a 401(k) into a Roth IRA at some point, and then leave that account to children or grandchildren, who can draw the money out tax-free—or, in turn, let the account grow even larger over time before transferring it, tax-free, to their heirs. (All this assumes, of course, that future governmental leaders don't come in and ruin a good thing, as governmental leaders are wont to do at times when they need access to tax revenues from the people.)

In fact, a Roth can be a fine tool for sheltering income you don't need in retirement. If you're forced to take distributions from another account, such as a traditional IRA, yet you don't need the cash to live on and you don't want to pay added taxes on the income that cash ultimately generates, you can funnel your distributions into a Roth IRA and leave them there for later use or for trailing generations to use one day. In this instance, you're not executing a rollover; you can't roll money from a taxable IRA into a nontaxable Roth. You're just taking the required minimum distributions, paying the required taxes, and then turning around and sticking the proceeds into the Roth.

Unfortunately, not all employers offer a Roth 401(k) option to employees, though the numbers are increasing. And like traditional IRAs, Roth IRAs impose various restrictions that limit your ability to contribute from one year to the next. Still, if you have access to one or the other or both, do yourself a favor and open an account. The next best thing to free money is tax-free money, and the Roth is one of the very few investments that offer that.

17

How Do I Bring All the Pieces Together?

What's the most important part of a flashlight? The light itself? The batteries? The casing? The electrical contacts that transfer energy from the batteries to the bulb?

No one part of a flashlight is any more essential than another. Ultimately, all the various pieces must work as a whole to serve a single purpose. A portfolio of investments should do the same. Stocks grow faster than the rate of inflation over time; that's important. Bonds provide income and stability; that's important. Cash offers ultimate safety of principal and the capital necessary to pursue opportunities; that's important.

Asset Allocation

The commingling of all the various assets groups that constitute a portfolio is what Wall Street and the financial profession call "asset allocation." This is possibly the most important aspect of investing. Because ultimately it's not a matter of what stock or bond or mutual fund you own, it's that you own a diversified mix that is appropriate to your age and tolerance for the price fluctuations inherent in any investment. You can own shares in the best-run companies in the world, but if stocks are out of favor because of severe inflation or a deep recession, then the best-run companies in the world aren't going to mean much to your portfolio because their shares will have been undercut by investors seeking better opportunities elsewhere.

The basic idea behind asset allocation is little different from the idea behind a scale (think: scales of justice). The two sides generally seek to balance each other. If stocks fall from grace, your bonds or commodities or gold or whatever will pick up the slack. Or it could be that as U.S. stocks fade from view, your international investments take the reins. In both cases, the downdraft in one asset class is offset by an updraft in another. Certainly, these aren't one-for-one moves, meaning a dollar lost in the United States will be replaced by a dollar gained in Europe. Investing is asymmetrical. You might lose a dollar in U.S. stocks, gain 35 cents in U.S. bonds, lose 84 cents in foreign stocks, and gain $1.19 in gold. Whatever the case, academic studies clearly show that a combination of assets works to lower a portfolio's overall risk while improving its overall returns, precisely why allocating your assets is important to your wealth.

Asset allocation is a highly personal endeavor. There's no one-size-fits-all model, because your underlying factors—risk tolerance and time horizon—are different from your neighbor's or your colleague's. Though I mention risk tolerance and time horizon as two distinct factors, in practical terms they are inextricably united.

Risk Tolerance/Time Horizon

Risk tolerance, in large part, is a function of your time horizon. The shorter the time before you need access to a sum of money, the less tolerant you will be of risk, even if you consider yourself a very tolerant investor when it comes to accepting risk. You can't afford the loss, so assuming the risk is foolish. However, the longer the period until you need the money, the more risk you should be willing to assume. Trading risk for time offers the greatest chance that your money will work as hard as possible to meet your needs one day.

Of course, those platitudes apply only in a perfect world, where logic determines investor actions and emotion is absent. But investors are inherently emotional, otherwise panics and manias wouldn't pervade the history of stocks and banks and tulips. Losing money, even if just on paper, can be mood altering, if not life altering; just as the experience of huge gains, even if just on paper, can breed unrealistic euphoria. Therein lies the problem. Investors suffer from near-term myopia, capable of seeing only what the recent past has wrought and mistakenly projecting those results onto the future, the upshot being that they fail to sell at the right moments and fail to buy at the right moments. More typically they buy when euphoria abounds, only to sell when pessimism is widespread.

During roaring bull markets, everyone swears they're risk tolerant, confidently buying the most aggressive, small-company stocks trading at valuations surpassing stalwarts like IBM or Coca-Cola, only to get kneecapped when the exuberance cracks and they suddenly realize they didn't sign up for this kind of pain. Then, in bear markets, everyone is so risk averse they refuse to acknowledge screaming values, only to miss the gains that ensue.

Both scenarios are precisely opposite the path you should pursue, and they highlight why asset allocation and the rebalancing I explained in Chapter 15 are so crucial to your investment success.

When investors are exuberant and bulls are running rampant in any asset class—stocks, bonds, houses—risk is at its apex, though no one is paying attention at that point. Look for the exit in those moments, an opportunity to reduce your exposure, to move onto the sidelines and await the fallout, when the values will re-emerge. Similarly, when investors are morosely bearish, when prices for some particular asset have plunged to a multiyear low, risk is generally near the trough, though again no one is paying attention. Look for the entrance, the opportunity to wade into the destruction and buy valuable assets at depressed prices. In Wall Street's world this is the contrarian investment strategy of "buying when there's blood in the streets."

By investing in multiple asset classes, you reduce the risk of market hysteria. Your highs won't be as high, nor your lows as low. Asset allocation is a smoothing mechanism.

Target Allocation

Figuring out how much to own of what asset sounds more complicated than it is in practice. And the goal isn't to determine precisely that you should hold 57 percent in U.S. stocks, 9 percent in foreign stocks, 28 percent in bonds, and 6 percent in cash. The goal is to ballpark your target allocations so that you are, for instance, 60 percent stocks, 30 percent bonds, 10 percent cash. Because markets gyrate continually, you're looking to stay within a range around each marker. One month your stocks might be 64 percent of your assets, while bonds are 29 percent and cash 7 percent. That's fine. It's expected, and you don't need to rush to immediately move your allocations back to your targets.

The Internet is chockablock with quizzes and tests purporting to help you determine your risk tolerance, but the best gauge is your own gut instinct. As the age-old question asks: Can you sleep at night if a market correction wipes away 50 percent of the value of your account?

Don't react to that question in knee-jerk fashion. Don't assume you could never stomach such pain, or that you easily could. Really think about it in the context of your life today, where you are, where you're headed, and how soon you expect to be there. You can answer quiz questions in any way you want to achieve some result you think you should be aiming for, or you might reflexively conclude there's no way you'd tolerate a big loss in your portfolio.

But only in the maw of a brutal market, when housing prices are tanking 30 percent or more, and the Dow Jones Industrial Average is swinging more than 1,000 points over the course of a day, as it did during the panic of October 2008, will you ever fully appreciate your true tolerance for risk. You might wring your hands frantically at the vast losses you're accumulating, because you're only now realizing you took on too much risk. Or you might take it all in stride, seeing the volatility as an opportunity to put additional cash to work in a beaten-up asset.

This is where "time horizon" is most important.

If you have no use for the money for ten or fifteen years or more, does it really matter that the asset is bouncing around in price right now? Fluctuating prices are the norm with most assets, and if you're not living off those assets at the moment, then rising prices won't increase your standard of living today, just as falling prices won't affect your ability to put food on the table or pay the mortgage. You might be more tolerant of risk than you realize.

By similar measures, you might be less tolerant of market risk than you suppose. If your financial needs are relatively close at hand for the money you've put at risk, within five or seven years, you can't afford to take as much risk as you might think you're capable of withstanding. You don't have much time to recoup losses, potentially affecting your lifestyle or quashing your ultimate plans for the money. In this case, fluctuating prices can take more of a toll on your finances and your psyche than you might imagine when times are good and asset prices are escalating.

With truly short-term money—the dollars you need for a down payment on a house, a new car, a child's college tuition that will arrive in five years or less—there's no debate. Stay away from any asset whose value could fall. Certain obligations require that you have 100 percent of your principal available for your specific need when that need arises. This is a situation where, no matter your risk tolerance, you can damage your finances if you pursue a risky strategy to grow your money more quickly, only to see it plunge in value just at the moment you need it.

Rebalancing

Though asset allocation doesn't require a great deal of time once you've established your targets and structured your portfolio to fit them, you do need to pay some attention to your portfolio as bull and bear markets swing and lurch over time. The movements can throw your allocations way off-target, and you can end up with too much or too little risk in your portfolio. During the late 1990s, when stocks roared ahead, many investors found their stock allocation had wildly escalated, while their bond exposure fell far below their comfort zone. When stocks cracked in the 2000 bear market, those people suffered as their overexposure to stocks and underexposure to bonds resulted in greater losses than they expected.

This is where asset allocation and the rebalancing I mentioned earlier converge. If you rebalance your portfolio regularly (roughly every year, maybe one of the first actions in the new year), you keep your allocations in line because you are selling down the asset class that has grown too large and adding to the class that has become too small.

As you age, though, you will likely need to adjust your allocations. The closer you move to retirement, the more stability and safety you want in your portfolio. That means an increasing exposure to bonds and cash. Don't completely move out of stocks, however, regardless of your age. Statistically, you're likely to spend a meaningful number of years in retirement, and you will need the portfolio growth that only stocks can offer. Bonds have to work much too hard to sustain a standard of living over the course of many years, and at some point they will be overrun, particularly as medical expenses escalate.

ASSET ALLOCATION

		Cash	Treasury Bonds	Corp. Bonds	Large Stocks	Midcap Stocks	Small Stocks	Foreign Stocks	Total
Short Term (1–3 years)	Conservative Risk	50%	40%	10%					100%
	Medium Risk	25%	50%	20%	5%				100%
	Aggressive Risk	10%	60%	20%	10%				100%
Medium Term (3–7 years)	Conservative Risk	5%	55%	20%	15%			5%	100%
	Medium Risk	5%	30%	20%	20%	10%	10%	5%	100%
	Aggressive Risk	2%	15%	15%	28%	15%	15%	10%	100%
Long Term (7 years +)	Conservative Risk	5%	30%	15%	35%	10%	5%	5%	100%
	Medium Risk	3%	15%	12%	45%	15%	5%	5%	100%
	Aggressive Risk	1%	4%	4%	50%	10%	10%	15%	100%

As a very general rule of thumb—let's call it a starting point, actually—there's the widely held allocation model in which you subtract your age from 100, and the resulting number is the percentage you should have allocated to stocks. A thirty-year-old, therefore, would have 70 percent in stocks and the remainder in bonds and a little cash. An eighty-year-old would have 20 percent in stocks.

Though the allocations in the table on the previous page are not allocations I advocate that everyone follow, I do want to share with you what a typical allocation of assets might look like for people of various risk tolerances and over different time horizons. Again, this isn't prescriptive advice. Instead, use this to benchmark against and tweak the model as necessary to fit your needs. I've included only seven very basic asset classes, but you could just as easily add others, including foreign bonds, gold, and real estate investment trusts.

Foreign bonds are for investors with a medium or long time horizon who are not conservative. Replace a small portion of the bond component of your portfolio with no more than 5 percent to 10 percent in foreign bonds—5 percent for the medium-risk investors; 10 percent for those of the aggressive-risk bent.

Real estate investment trusts, or REITs, would fit into a portfolio with any time horizon, but these are mainly for investors with an appetite for medium or aggressive risk. Those with a short to medium time horizon should put no more than 5 percent in REITs. Those with the longest time to invest can go as much as 15 percent to 20 percent in REITs depending upon your risk tolerance. This allocation would largely come out of your allocations to cash and bonds, because while REITs are equities that trade on the stock market, they tend not to be well correlated with the broader stock-market moves, and they generally pay respectably large dividends because of their legal structure, thus replacing some of the interest income you'd otherwise generate off cash and bonds.

Finally, gold. This is a hedging instrument, and gold prices can be quite volatile. The most aggressive short-term investors could hold a 2 percent to 5 percent position in gold. Those with a longer time horizon and a more aggressive tolerance for risk can own between 10 percent and 20 percent, depending upon your personal view of the economy and the U.S. dollar. As I noted in Chapter 10 gold moves higher when inflation flares up or when the dollar loses value. The more you're worried about either event, the more you'd want in gold. It pays no income while you hold it, so it is not a direct replacement for cash or bonds. More likely, you should reduce your allocation to stocks, since gold's volatility is more in line with equities. Plus, amid inflation, equities will likely underperform, giving a real shine to gold.

18

Should I Invest Only in U.S. Companies?

The United States might reign as the world's largest stock market, but it's certainly not the world's only stock market. As capitalism in some form or another has spread across the globe since the fall of Communism, stock markets have sprouted from Côte d'Ivoire to Slovenia to Oman. Investment opportunity now exists all across the globe.

U.S. investors don't pay much attention to that fact and generally don't own nearly enough exposure to the rest of the world. The United States, after all, represents between a quarter and a fifth of the world's GDP in 2009, while U.S. investors generally place between 80 percent and 100 percent of their assets in America. That doesn't mean you should rush to invest in such places as Slovenia and Oman. But given that many parts of the world are growing substantially faster than the United States, and given that many economies and many currencies are stronger, some portion of a well-diversified portfolio needs to be in foreign markets. Foreign investment will help protect your portfolio and your purchasing power over time as other economies grow and as other currencies rise in value against the dollar.

You will regularly hear that investing overseas is too risky. But that's like saying "dogs are brown"—it's true sometimes, but not every time. Many of the world's developed markets are no more risky than the United States market. These would include markets in places like Australia, Singapore, Japan, England, Germany, and other Western European countries. These markets share with the United States many similar regulations and accounting conventions and rules of law. Yet by locating some of your money there, you are taking part in the growth of companies that are not necessarily tied to the U.S. economy. That's diversification. You're moving away from the dollar, away from the U.S. economy, and away from U.S. markets.

Emerging and Frontier Markets

When you venture beyond the developed markets, you enter emerging markets and, farther down the ladder, frontier markets. Here you will find greater risks, though also commensurately greater returns, given how small some of these markets are and how rapidly they can move. The most widely known among the emerging markets are the so-called BRIC countries of Brazil, Russia, India, and China, four of the largest, fastest-growing second-tier economies in the world. Brazil and Russia are big natural-resource-base countries, while India and China are big players in manufacturing, services, and the consumerism, which naturally shadows a population that combined exceeds two billion people.

Amid the global credit crisis and market collapse in 2008, overseas markets fell apart, often sliding much farther than the U.S. market. Much of that fall was a function of the asset-price inflation spurred by years of Federal Reserve policy that kept U.S. interest rates unrealistically low, which, in turn, encouraged investors all over the world to seek better returns in other assets, such as stocks. When the crisis hit, the leverage unwound and markets globally sank.

But that's likely to prove temporary, particularly over the longer term. Much of the unwinding came from professional money managers who dumped stocks and other assets to meet margin calls (meaning they'd borrowed to buy shares and had to sell them to raise cash). Moreover, investors sold anything and everything to rush into the safety of U.S. dollars. Economies overseas aren't going to stop growing because the United States slows down. True, the U.S. economy, particularly the U.S. consumer, is clearly an important factor in the growth of overseas economies, but America is no longer *the* sole engine of growth. It's one of several engines. As it moves onto a different track, other economies will continue motoring ahead because of other factors.

Countries throughout Asia, Oceania, Africa, and parts of Europe and Latin America continue marching toward urbanization and Western standards, which continue fueling growing consumer demand and a pressing desire to build up necessary infrastructure. The knock-on effect is that countries will begin turning their efforts more toward other markets, decoupling to some degree from the United States, despite the misplaced claims that decoupling is a dead concept in the wake of the market crash.

Simple Routes to Foreign Investment

You want to become a part of that process by allocating part of your assets to foreign securities, particularly stocks. The easiest path is U.S.-based mutual funds and exchange-trade funds, or American Depositary Receipts, known as ADRs. Funds and ETFs come in all varieties, from basic, international funds that own broad exposure to the world, to highly concentrated funds that own exposure to a single country. ADRs, meanwhile, are U.S.-listed shares of foreign companies from a wide range of countries big and small.

Good opportunities exist in picking ADRs, but you need the temperament necessary to own individual stocks, and the talent for picking the good from the bad. If you'd rather leave that to the pros, then I suggest you focus on mutual funds and ETFs. And I would encourage you to own a broad-based international fund as your primary overseas investment, and to spice that up a bit with a small stake in a regional fund specifically targeting Asia, which is clearly emerging as the world's growth engine. If you're really risk tolerant, you might consider a China fund, but be warned: Chinese stock markets are the epitome of volatility.

For investors who want overseas exposure without the corporate risk inherent in stocks, but seek better returns than are available through the foreign currency CDs and savings accounts I mentioned previously, look at foreign bond funds. Basic funds invest in the sovereign debt of developed countries and, aside from currency risk, are generally no more risky than U.S. bond funds. Other funds offer the higher yields of emerging nations, and a small portion can juice your overall returns, but you must be aware of the greater risk of defaults and currency blowups.

At the end of the day, the United States will remain the world's premier economy. But other economies are climbing the ladder, and any twenty-first-century portfolio must be hitched to them to benefit from that growth.

19

How Much Do I Need for Retirement?

That's the number everyone wants to know. Peg that and you can plan precisely for retirement. You'll know your spending needs, you can predict annual income with greater precision, and you'll know how long your money will last based upon how you invest—and if that period isn't long enough, you'll know how to tweak it to stretch your dollars farther.

The Number: A Misguided Quest

Unfortunately, The Number is not a real number. It doesn't exist, because there's no possible way to determine your true cost of living years from now. There's no way to determine exactly how much you'll be able to save between now and then because there is no way to know what expenses and challenges will pop up in your life, from an additional child to a medical malady to the loss of a job. You have no idea how your life might change over the years, or how your wants today may become the necessities of tomorrow and vice-versa. You can't begin to predict your health needs, how healthcare will change, or the costs associated with keeping you alive and active, or at least well cared for. There's no way to calculate the actual returns you'll earn on your cash, your stocks, or your bonds, and there's no possible means of knowing how the economy of tomorrow will look: inflation, deflation, stagflation, recession, depression, above-average growth. Every one of those plus so many other variables directly affects the size of your ultimate nest egg and the ultimate costs you will one day confront.

Despite the many, many worksheets and media articles and books that purport to tell you how to determine how much you need to save today to afford your life tomorrow, the calculations rely on so many unknowns that, at the end of the exercise, the number you wind up with remains just a guesstimate.

There's certainly nothing wrong with a guesstimate. The human mind works best when it at least has something supposedly concrete to work toward. So having some sort of goal to aim for is better than having no goal at all.

But here's my ultimate message: The Number really isn't important. The Number is not the answer. In fact, "How much do I need to save?" isn't even the right question.

The *real* question is, "How do I ensure that I'm content in retirement?"

Contentedness is more than money. It's the feeling of fulfillment, the ability to live your retirement on your terms instead of feeling trapped in a retirement you don't want but have no way of escaping. And the key to contentedness isn't necessarily the money—it's the planning.

A groundbreaking study in 2002 by AIG SunAmerica surveyed people who have been in retirement for several years and found that those who are happiest in their golden years are the ones who planned the longest. That doesn't imply they have the most money. Sometimes they don't, though clearly they end up with larger balances simply by dint of having saved for so long.

Nevertheless, the survey found that retirement success, retirement happiness, is the byproduct of two leading factors: the amount of time spent saving and asset diversification. The happiest retirees saved, on average, for twenty-four years, stashing money regularly in 401(k) plans and IRAs and holding investments ranging from mutual funds and individual stocks to bonds and, to a lesser degree, real estate. Those who rated themselves unhappiest spent less than half that time saving, rarely contributed to retirement-savings accounts, and were never focused on buying stocks or bonds or mutual funds. Indeed, a quarter of those who labeled themselves the must unfulfilled retirees basically invested in nothing.

So retirement isn't about The Number. It's about *any* number. It's about starting today and regularly saving for tomorrow. It's about making the most of the 401(k) plans and IRAs you have at your disposal and diversifying your assets so that you can weather the inevitable storms along the way. Obviously, doing this means you will accumulate a nest egg. But more important, it means a far greater likelihood that you will reach retirement happy with your preparations and comfortably content with the money you do have.

20

How Do I Insure My Future?

The Boy Scout motto is overused, but I'll use it anyway because it is so apt: Be Prepared.

Bad things happen to good finances all the time, and the only way to protect yourself and your family is to protect your financial assets from being wiped out by a catastrophe. That means insurance in some form: life, health, auto, home, annuities, just to name a few major types of policies. For a relatively small fee—the annual premium—an insurer agrees to shoulder a substantially larger risk than you can afford, promising to step in and cover the costs of certain events that otherwise threaten to destroy your finances. Do you have enough cash on hand to pay a judgment against you should your car happen to be involved in an accident that kills or maims someone? If not, you need auto insurance and maybe a so-called umbrella policy. Do you have the cash available to rebuild your house if a disaster destroys it tomorrow? If not, you need a homeowner's policy. Do you have enough money to guarantee your ability to live in retirement for as many as thirty or forty years (and, remember, centenarians are one of the fastest-growing demographics in America)? If not, you might consider annuities and long-term care policies that guarantee an income and cash for extended care for as long as you continue to breathe, no matter how long that is.

Insurance for many people is a necessary evil, a hassle that requires the payment of a bunch of money for a service few expect to use. But that's a misguided way to consider insurance. No one ever complains about their taxes' paying the salaries of firefighters and policemen because everyone knows that in an emergency you want those first responders available to help protect your life. Insurance is identical. It's the first responder of the financial world, there to protect your assets.

Some forms of insurance are mandatory, such as a homeowner's policy that a lender will require if you buy your house using a mortgage. Other forms aren't mandatory but are clearly a necessity, such as life insurance once you have a family. And still other forms of insurance are neither mandatory nor necessary, but they're nevertheless an excellent way to protect your future, such as an annuity that can ease the financial worries you might harbor about old age and the possibility that you may run out of cash one day.

The problem with insurance of any kind is that figuring out exactly how much coverage you need and what deductibles are right for you can be numbingly complex, or just numbing. Buy too little coverage, and the risks that you and your family are exposed to still threaten your assets. Buy too much and you're just wasting money on the premiums. Agree to the various policy riders that insurers pitch and you can find out after the fact that the rider did little to benefit you. But skipping every rider means missing out on some benefits that can make a policy markedly more useful.

Life Insurance

One in three Americans does not have life insurance.

That fact comes from a 2008 survey commissioned by Heritage Union, a life-insurance company, so possibly it's skewed. Then again, survey after survey has shown through the years that Americans are largely an underinsured lot when it comes to protecting their family in the event a breadwinner dies.

That's the role of life insurance, though really a better term for this type of coverage might be *salary* insurance, since life insurance isn't so much about insuring your life as it is about insuring a breadwinner's salary.

When a working spouse dies before retirement, families too often struggle with a shock to their financial system. Costs that once seemed easily affordable can suddenly seem quite dear when the income that helped support the family no longer exists. The straits are all the more dire if the deceased spouse was the family's only breadwinner. All that was normal is no more, and plans that you two shared for your future and your children's future can evaporate.

To be sure, not every American needs life insurance, for one reason or another. But many of those who don't have it do need it, and according to surveys, the excuses they offer for not buying coverage range from claims that policies are too expensive to a feeling that life insurance is unnecessary to a sense that shopping for a policy is too much of a hassle. For people who fall into any of those categories, here's some news: Life insurance is cheaper than you think; you do need coverage, particularly if you're married or have children; and shopping doesn't have to be any more difficult than picking out a new pair of shoes.

You just need to understand what you need and why you need it.

Term and Whole Life

Life insurance comes in two forms: term insurance and permanent insurance, more commonly known as "whole life." As you might deduce from the self-explanatory titles, term insurance remains in force for a set number of years, while whole life sticks with you for your whole life, assuming you continue to pay the premiums. Though the basic premise is identical—to pay heirs a sum of money upon the insured person's death—these policies are drastically different.

The permutations of whole-life policies and the variations on those permutations are too numerous to discuss in this book. Moreover, while whole life can serve certain, highly specific situations very well, it is often too much policy for the average family. What you need to understand about whole life is this: The policies are sharply more expensive than term life, meaning you get less coverage for more money. You do get a savings component with whole life that can be attractive to some consumers chronically incapable of saving, but the reality is that you will find more lucrative savings options outside a whole life policy.

Insurance is not about saving. You're insuring against a particular risk, in this case the risk of premature death that hampers a family's ability to afford key costs such as housing, college tuition for the kids, or even a retirement nest egg for a surviving spouse. From a pure insurance perspective, you can't go wrong with basic term-life insurance.

Term life is in place for a specific term, usually ten to thirty years, though some policies stretch a bit longer. Your goal is to insure your family's income for the time during which you have exposure to a known risk. The risk of not having enough to provide for a child's education is in place from the moment that child is born until college graduation. The risk that your family won't have enough money to stay in the family's home in the event some accident erases your income is in place for generally as long as your mortgage is outstanding.

With life insurance, you are basically seeking to replace lost income. Period. And the great benefit of term life is that it is relatively cheap. As I write this, a thirty-year-old, nonsmoking male in my home state of Virginia could buy $250,000 of term-life coverage for about $230 a year through one of the country's highly rated insurers. With a whole-life policy, that cost more than quadruples to nearly $1,000 a year.

The downside to term life is that it vanishes when the term

expires, and if you still need coverage, your costs will rise. Thirty years later, if that thirty-year-old male still required coverage, a fifteen-year policy would cost about $865 annually in today's dollars. Now, that doesn't take into account inflation or changing mortality statistics that could easily alter the price structure for life insurance three decades from now. Nevertheless it offers an example of how your insurance costs might change and shows that even at an older age you're still paying less than you would have been paying all along for permanent insurance.

One of the long-standing rules of thumb with insurance holds that you should "buy term and invest the difference." In other words, buy enough term insurance to cover your family's needs, and then invest the difference between the premiums you pay for the term policy and the premiums you would have paid had you purchased a whole-life policy instead. You are, in effect, creating a hybrid version of a whole-life contract, only you're likely able to generate greater investment returns on your own than would accrue inside the insurance contract because the options are much broader outside the policy. Though there are clearly circumstances when this rule won't apply, it's a rule that will serve most families well.

Who Needs Coverage?

If you have children you need life insurance. If you're married and your spouse doesn't work, you need life insurance. Basically, if you serve as the primary source of financial support for anyone in your life, then you need life insurance.

Perhaps the biggest challenge with any form of life insurance is figuring out how much insurance you need. Here again, the financial world has its rule of thumb. In this case, the rule says you need between five and ten times your annual, after-tax salary (after-tax because you're looking to replace the money you actually bring home, and since insurance payouts are tax-free you have no need to replace the portion of your salary that went to taxes). But here I don't necessarily agree with the rule. It's fairly simplistic and doesn't take into account specific family needs.

Here's what I mean. If you earn, let's say, $60,000 a year after tax, then a simple five-or-ten-times-your-income calculation would yield life insurance needs of between $300,000 and $600,000. But what if you have a $250,000 mortgage on your house and twin toddlers for whom you want to pay college costs seventeen years from now at roughly $177,000 a year each (that inflation-adjusted national average comes from a college-cost-planning calculator at www.troweprice.com), and you have a spouse to whom you'd like to leave at least $200,000 to help seed a nest egg in the event you die prematurely. You're already at $804,000 in coverage, well above the rule of thumb. Or what happens if you have a special-needs child or sibling for whom you want to leave enough money to provide lifelong care?

I am cherrypicking a bit in creating those examples, no doubt. Still, it makes the point that every family's financial needs are different, and they can't always be shoehorned into a compact rule of thumb.

To better gauge your needs, determine what costs you want your policy to cover and then tally them up. Those costs might include the aforementioned mortgage payoff, college costs, and the seed capital for a nest egg, but they could just as easily include an emergency fund for your family to draw on, living expenses that the deceased spouse's income would have helped cover, or any other special costs specific to your family.

Clearly, you don't want too much insurance, because chances are you will never use it, and you will have simply wasted money. However, you also don't want too little, since that could leave your family struggling financially in the wake of an untimely death.

Homeowner's and Auto Insurance

For most homeowners and drivers, insurance on your house and car is mandatory.

That's because if you have a mortgage on your house or a loan on your car, the lender will require that you carry enough coverage to replace the house or the car in the event of a catastrophe. The lender isn't so worried about you, honestly, as much as it's worried about protecting its investment in your property. If the house or car is destroyed, lenders want assurance that you will have the money to repay what you owe, or to replace the property and continue making the required monthly payments.

With cars, states get involved as well by mandating a minimum amount of coverage. Their rationale: They know that without such laws, an unhealthy portion of the population would skip auto insurance altogether and thereby present a liability to other motorists and the healthcare system in the event the uninsured driver causes a crash that damages or destroys another driver's vehicle or, worse, sends that driver to the hospital. It should not be incumbent upon the innocent driver—or the innocent driver's insurer—to repair or replace the damaged car to foot the medical bills.

Whatever you do with auto and home insurance, don't skimp on coverage. If you can only afford the absolute state minimums required for auto insurance, then fine, that's your only option. But to the degree you can, pay up for greater coverage. Though you will pay a slightly larger premium, the heftier coverage will protect you better if you end up in a car accident, particularly if it is one that seriously injures someone and the smashup is your fault. Greater coverage reduces the likelihood that someone you hurt will come after your personal assets as recompense for their injuries, for their medical bills, and to replace their vehicle. The minimums associated with state-mandated coverage may not adequately compensate the injured, in which case your assets are suddenly in the line of fire.

Indeed, your car is the biggest liability in your life. Your house isn't likely to cause a death or dismemberment in a moment when you're not paying attention. Your car is. Therefore, you want as much coverage as you can afford to adequately protect your assets against your own negligence. And remember this: You can be sued even if the wreck isn't your fault. You might be stopped at a light and someone plows into you, but you, in turn, hit an old lady crossing the street. You will be pulled into that lawsuit for failure to maintain control.

The appropriate amount of auto coverage depends on the value of the assets you own. If you have a house worth $200,000 and another $50,000 in investments, then coverage that exceeds $250,000 per accident is where you should start. If you have few assets that would be exposed to loss in a liability lawsuit, then the state minimums where you live are likely sufficient. And if you have a large base of assets, then consider an "umbrella policy" as a rider on your auto-insurance contract. A standard umbrella policy covers liabilities up to $1 million, and generally for less than $300 a year, often much less, depending on where you live and the insurance company underwriting your policy. You can tack on additional coverage in $1 million increments for an even smaller annual premium.

Auto policies are divided into liability (to pay for damages to the person and property of third parties) and comprehensive collision (to cover damage to your car from an accident, including such things as glass breakage from a minor incident). Costs for collision and comprehensive coverage are usually quite high. Requesting a higher deductible on these policies can be a wise financial move that will lower your premiums dramatically. Added to the collision policy should be family medical coverage for accidents involving yourself and your family. This coverage is very cheap—about $150 for $300,000 coverage—and is a very prudent purchase.

With homeowner's insurance, meanwhile, one of the mistakes home buyers make is basing their coverage on the purchase price of the house. Likely this will sound strange, but your purchase doesn't represent the value of your house. The purchase price you paid includes the value of the land, and in some jurisdictions around the country, particularly along the coasts and in highly desirable neighborhoods in certain key cities, the land's value far exceeds the price of the physical structure on it. Paying premiums to cover the purchase price, then, would be a waste of money, since in a disaster you don't have to replace the land, just the building.

To be sure, your lender might balk, since it will want assurance that you will have the financial wherewithal to repay the outstanding mortgage balance if your house is destroyed. Thus, your lender might not allow you to carry insurance for less than the value of your mortgage, though some will. However, for those who do not have a mortgage, you're free to carry as much or as little insurance as you wish.

For a more accurate gauge of how much insurance you really need, pay a few hundred dollars to have your house fully appraised. An appraisal is necessary, because in a situation in which your house must be rebuilt, it suddenly becomes a custom home, even if you're rebuilding a tract house in a neighborhood of cookie-cutter homes. When builders build out a neighborhood, they buy everything in bulk and lock in prices much lower than you'll have to pay to rebuild a single house. What's more, homes often change over time as you remodel. Out goes an outdated kitchen, in comes a more modern kitchen with upscale counters and cabinets and appliances. That changes the cost to rebuild your home.

Some of the better insurers nowadays rely on "total component estimating" to determine the real cost of replacing your home. This method takes into account the materials that compose your house, since those materials can be different from the materials of your neighbor's house. Insurers that simply calculate the cost per square foot to rebuild a home like yours can leave you holding a policy that does not adequately cover the true costs you might one day confront.

To further protect your finances, make sure your homeowner's policy includes a replacement-value clause. These clauses stipulate that the insurer will pay a sum above what your policy states. Guaranteed-replacement value was once the gold standard, promising to pay whatever it cost to rebuild your house after you met the deductible. Those policies are still around, but they are increasingly rare and exceedingly expensive.

More common today are the limited-replacement value policies that promise to pay either 120 percent or 125 percent of the stated policy coverage. So, for instance, if your policy covers $200,000, your insurer will actually pay as much as $250,000 to rebuild your home. Just be certain that such a clause is part of your contract, and be wary of clauses that promise "fair market" value or "cash value" coverage. Under these clauses, your insurer will deduct wear and tear and depreciation on the possessions you replace, effectively reducing your coverage. Worse, you'll probably have to prove that you owned the item and its cost when it was lost or destroyed—and that can be a real hassle in a housing emergency.

To keep your premiums as low as possible, consider a higher deductible. Homeowner's insurance often starts with a $500 deductible, though you can request $1,000 or a certain percentage of the policy's coverage amount that you're willing to foot first. For instance, on that $200,000 policy I mentioned a moment ago, you might be willing to pay the first 1 percent of any claims, the equivalent of $2,000. If so, your premiums will come down fairly sharply. Just be sure you can actually afford the deductible. You might be gambling that nothing of consequence will happen to your house, or you might be expecting that you will put into a savings account the premium dollars you save that you can then use to pay that larger deductible one day, but if ultimately you can't afford several thousand dollars, for whatever reason, you are going to have a very difficult time getting the necessary repairs done.

Finally, every few years you should make it a point to shop your insurance policies again. Rates change all the time on home, auto, and life insurance policies in particular as new insurers enter a market or as existing insurers seek a different book of business. Insurers at those moments are particularly competitive and you will often find better rates for the same or even improved coverage. Yes, it can be a hassle, but when you can save a few hundred dollars a year or more, the payoff can be worth the effort.

Annuities

Though widely sold as an investment product, annuities are actually a form of insurance. You relinquish to an insurer a sum of money and, in return, the insurer guarantees to pay you a certain amount of income over a predetermined period or, in many instances, until you stop breathing. Investments never make such guarantees; only insurance products and FDIC-backed bank accounts do.

For good reason, though, annuities have a bad reputation. Many annuity peddlers are modern-day snake-oil salesmen who care only about fattening their own paycheck, regardless of the risks and financial disaster the sale of an annuity can impose on buyers. Most often those buyers are the elderly who are too easily manipulated by fast-talking hucksters not above lying about the product they're pitching, or using fearmongering to insinuate that seniors risk losing their nest egg to some nebulous peril that doesn't exist. For that reason, state and federal regulators in recent years have been cracking down on abusive annuity sales tactics, particularly related to so-called variable annuities and index annuities.

Dubious sales practices aside, certain annuities can have a place in a well-diversified nest egg. Better yet, they can provide a base level of income in retirement that you can never outlive. That last clause, "never outlive," can be more important than you realize. Given life-enhancing medical improvements, life in retirement could be longer than you ever expect, and you never want to face the worry that you might one day run out of money. An annuity can permanently erase those worries.

But not just any annuity will do.

For retirees, in particular, an immediate, fixed annuity is where you want to concentrate your dollars. That's because immediate annuities are designed to provide you an income immediately. With an immediate annuity you are trading some portion of your nest egg for the promise of a set amount of monthly income. As with a savings account or a CD, the return you earn on an immediate annuity is generally fixed, though some do offer variable returns if you don't mind the risk that your monthly income could rise or fall from month to month. Annuities regularly generate more money that you'd earn by owning savings accounts or even long-term CDs. That's because annuity payments include both the return on your investment and a portion of your original principal. And there's no risk of the insurer reducing your payment once your original principal has been completely returned; that's the risk the insurer takes in underwriting the contract.

The most important benefit of an immediate annuity is that the contract allows you to structure a payment schedule that can last a set number of years, or, as I noted a few paragraphs back, until you die. Annuities are a fine way to create a sense of financial security in retirement that can ease your mind because you know that, at the every least, you will always have some level of income above your Social Security check, even if your nest egg is fully depleted. In effect, you are buying insurance against outliving your nest egg.

Many strategies exist for incorporating an annuity into a retirement portfolio, but one that makes a great deal of sense to me is this: Use an annuity along with whatever Social Security check you receive to fund your necessary monthly expenses. Then, use whatever other income the rest of your nest egg generates to fund your discretionary spending. With this approach, your basic costs of living are never in question, because the permanent income from the annuity and your Social Security check will cover those expenses.

The key risk is that your cost of living could accelerate at a sharp pace, particularly because of healthcare, and fixed annuities generally don't offer inflation adjustment, though that is changing within the industry. There are ways to deal with this, however. A long-term care policy can help manage the costs of aging when you are incapable to caring for yourself at home (see the next chapter). As for escalating costs of living, you can ladder your annuities (much like the practice of laddering CDs I mentioned in a previous chapter) to generate greater income as inflation rises.

Annuities are interest-rate and age sensitive. The higher the prevailing interest rates are at any given point, and the older you are, the greater the monthly income you receive from the contract. You can use that to your advantage. Instead of investing at once the entire sum earmarked for annuities, spread the purchases across several different annuities over time. At age sixty-five, for example, put 60 percent to 70 percent of your annuity money into a contract that will pay out over your remaining lifetime. Then, at seventy, you put another 10 percent or 15 percent into a second annuity that pays over a ten- or fifteen-year period. Finally, at seventy-five, you fund a third immediate annuity with the remaining sum that pays out over ten years. In doing so, you're locking in guaranteed income for as long as you live, and you're giving yourself a cost-of-living raise every few years and capturing any increase in interest rates. The reason annuities numbers two and three aren't structured for lifetime payout is that you'll receive more money by taking the cash over a specific period. Moreover, you will generally reach a point in retirement where your basic costs begin to go down, not up. Your travel and entertaining taper off, your hobbies wane, and you're just not spending as much as you did in the earlier years. Those savings along with the bump up in pay from the additional annuities will help you manage the higher costs that do pop up elsewhere in your budget.

Of course, this is just one example of how you might build an annuity ladder. You can build them in any way that best fits your need. My point is simply that using multiple annuities can help you navigate potential worries that can arise if inflation becomes a real concern in your personal economy.

However you ultimately decide to employ annuities, don't dump all of your nest egg into one. At most, put 20 percent to, maybe, 25 percent of your retirement cash into an annuity program. The reason: Once you annuitize a sum of money, you can't reclaim those dollars except through the stream of monthly payments the insurer returns to you over time. Thus, if you suddenly need a lump sum of cash for an emergency, your annuity will not serve you well at all. In an emergency, you will want money in stocks or bonds or savings that you can tap into immediately.

Moreover, once you annuitize, your money is no longer growing. This echoes the point I made about inflation a moment ago. Your money is slowly being disbursed to you in equal payments; it's not being invested for growth. Yet even in retirement you need some measure of growth to help keep pace with some measure of inflation. Again, you will want that money in investments that are growing in value, particularly stocks.

What you generally do not want in retirement is a variable annuity. These are too often the bad kinds of annuities. Variable annuities are designed to help accumulate additional wealth, meaning they are best employed before retirement, and then only by workers who have maxed out their allowable contributions to a 401(k) plan and an IRA and still have additional money they want to invest for retirement on a tax-deferred basis. Once you hit retirement, however, you're generally not in wealth-accumulation mode. You have instead reached the phase of life where you're living off the assets you already accumulated during your working career. You are in asset-preservation mode. And in that phase, variable annuities can be very destructive. If you plunk the bulk of your nest egg into a variable annuity at sixty-five or older—as many annuity hucksters want retirees to do—and the stock market crashes (as happened in 2008), you might not have enough years remaining to repair the financial damage the market wrought on your account. Your quality of life in retirement could suffer, and your ability to fund medical cost or long-term care expenses could be severely compromised. As such, buying a variable annuity in retirement is, rule of thumb, a bad idea.

Keep in mind that insurers can fail. Several have through the years. So your policy is only as strong as the insurer that stands behind it. As with any form of insurance, then, you want an annuity from the strongest insurers, generally those with a rating of "A" or above. You'll find ratings posted at the ratings-agencies' websites: Moody's Investors Service (www.moodys.com), A.M. Best (www.ambest.com), and Standard & Poor's (www.standardandpoors.com). If your insurer does happen to fail, all is not lost when it comes to your annuity. State laws require that, in an insurance company liquidation, annuity owners be paid first and in full before other creditors receive the first nickel. If the insurance company doesn't have enough money, state guaranty associations that are funded by other insurance companies make good on the annuity contracts.

21

How Do I Pay for Care in My Old Age?

In a world where people are living longer and the cost of providing the necessary care is growing at a rate far faster than overall inflation, I am convinced that long-term care insurance might be one of the smartest investments anyone makes. Indeed, while your portfolio will fund your retirement, a long-term care policy might just save it.

LTC, as this type of insurance is commonly known, is a policy that helps pay the expenses of old age, everything from the monthly expenses at an assisted-living center or nursing home to the costs of hiring a family member to provide transportation to the doctor's office. Many, many people mistakenly assume that Medicare, Medicaid, and traditional healthcare policies will pay these costs. They generally don't. Medicare, for instance, pays for no more than 100 days of long-term care costs, such as the costs of nursing-home care, but that's well short of the roughly two years that the average retiree will spend needing some form of long-term care. Medicaid does cover some long-term care expenses, but access is limited to those who are effectively impoverished. Healthcare policies don't cover long-term at all.

The costs involved can scramble your nest egg. A 2008 study by MetLife, the big insurance company, reported that the average nursing home costs about $77,000 a year, while assisted-living centers run about $36,000 annually. The cost of providing in-home care runs about $20 an hour, the equivalent of $58,000 a year for eight hours of daily care. Remember: Those are today's dollars. Inflate that out a decade or so at between 6 percent and 8 percent a year and you're talking about monstrous costs.

Your family's retirement portfolio might ultimately be capable of handling the expense, but at what cost to a surviving spouse? Will that spouse be able to live as comfortably if the family's money is effectively eliminated by the other partner's long-term care costs?

Because these costs come out of your pocket, an LTC policy helps preserve the assets that otherwise would be siphoned off to pay eldercare expenses.

But Will You Need Coverage?

That's the question everyone asks when considering whether to buy an LTC policy, and because the costs can be exceedingly high, potential buyers often look at their future through rose-hued glasses and presume that they're going to be among the people who won't need long-term care. But here's a statistic to consider as you read this section: 62 percent of people over the age of eighty-five will require help with one or more of the activities of daily living—eating, bathing, dressing, toileting, and so on—according to the American Council of Life Insurers.

Like life insurance, LTC contracts provide coverage up to whatever amount you specify, usually expressed in terms of the "daily benefit" over some specific period of time. You might, for instance, opt for $150 a day in coverage for up to three years, or, if you want absolute assurance you will always be covered no matter how long you live, you can choose an unlimited duration, so that you receive your daily benefit for as long as required. (For the record, you will often read in popular financial and consumer publications that the average length of stay in a nursing home is two and a half years, but that is a near-meaningless statistic, because you could require assisted-living or home-health care for years before moving into a nursing home. Moreover, averages, by definition, mean lots of people are above and below the norm, so, again, you're really just guessing.)

How much coverage you ultimately need and for how long is a bit of a guess. Clearly, no one has a clue how long they might require care later in life, and equally difficult is knowing what that care will cost. MassMutual operates a website at www.notaburden .com that provides a state-by-state breakdown on today's long-term care costs, and that can provide a good measure to gauge how much coverage you need.

Recognize, of course, that those costs will increase over time, so you will want an LTC policy that provides for inflation protection. Be sure to choose the inflation protection that compounds each year. Some just increase each year at, say, 5 percent of the original daily benefit, meaning your $150 daily benefit increases by $7.50 each year. With a policy that compounds, your benefit increases by $7.50 in Year 1, $7.88 in Year 2, $8.27 in Year 3, and so on. By Year 10, a policy that does not compound will pay $225 a day, while one that does compound will pay up to $244.33 a day. Over the course of a year, that's more than $7,000 in additional benefits.

LTC policies can be quite expensive, depending on your age when you first purchase a policy. Cost can range as high as $6,000 a year if you buy a policy in the late sixties, say, when retirees start really contemplating the costs they might face as old age closes in. Buying when you're younger, in your early fifties or even your forties, is sharply less expensive, often less than $1,000 annually. The added benefit of buying earlier is that you face a smaller risk of being denied coverage. Unlike health or life insurance, where a pre-existing condition simply means you pay more for coverage, LTC is a pass-fail policy. If you have a pre-existing condition, you fail, and you won't be able to purchase a policy. You're much less likely to have those conditions when you're younger, and, thus, won't be prevented from buying coverage. For that reason, your fifties are often the best time to buy a policy. Your health is still generally good and the premiums are still generally affordable. Older than that, and you risk failing the test, negating your ability to obtain coverage. Younger, and you will pay more at the risk of never needing the policy, meaning you've pumped tens of thousands of dollars into a contract that is effectively useless. Still, many people in their forties are buyers of LTC policies because the rates are so low that they can lock in a desirable benefit at affordable prices.

Though LTC policies can be highly beneficial, they're not for everyone. Those who retire with a nest egg exceeding several million dollars are effectively self-insured. Your assets will cover your needs and an LTC policy generally makes little sense—although it can be a way to preserve a larger inheritance for heirs, if that's an important factor to you. On the other end of the spectrum, people who retire with relatively few assets should not spend their money on LTC premiums because you will, in all likelihood, qualify for state and federal programs that will pay your basic, long-term care costs. If you're in that group, you're better off diverting into an investment program the money you'd use for LTC premiums. That will provide you with greater income to live on in retirement before any long-term care needs arise.

In short, LTC policies are often best for people who expect to accumulate retirement assets of between about $500,000 and roughly $2 million. You have the assets to live on comfortably in retirement, but you're also at risk of losing that cushion quickly if long-term care needs force you to begin drawing down your savings faster than you expected.

One of the more confusing components of long-term care is the so-called elimination period. This functions exactly like the deductible on your homeowner's policy. This is the amount of money you must pay from your own pocket before your LTC policy kicks in. For whatever reasons, consumers have been trained mentally to choose the lowest deductible possible, thinking it best to pay as little as necessary from their own wallet. But that's not always the smartest strategy. Higher deductibles lower your premiums. Moreover, insurance is designed to cover a catastrophe. Then money for relatively small expenses should come from personal savings, with insurance picking up only the truly large events that would otherwise undermine your financial stability. That's particularly true with an LTC.

To a certain degree, the costs of aging are part of the reason your nest egg exists, so you should expect your savings to help fund some of the expenses. An LTC policy should step in just when your costs threaten to spiral beyond your means. You have to define for yourself what "catastrophic" means, since different people will have different means and different needs.

Elimination periods typically stretch from thirty days to one year, with many buyers opting for sixty- or ninety-day elimination periods. That's a bit too short to my way of thinking. Periods of 180 days to a year often make more sense, because the premiums are markedly lower, saving you thousands of dollars over time that can help cover those early costs before the policy kicks in.

The biggest concern with LTC policies is that the premiums are generally not guaranteed, meaning you might start out paying $1,500 a year, but then, several years later, your insurer dispatches a letter announcing it is jacking up rates to $3,000 a year or more, possibly well beyond your ability to pay. Obviously, that can be unsettling, and, indeed, many consumers have purchased LTCs only to find this exact scenario has come to pass. It stems from the early days of LTC contracts, when insurers, in their rush to compete for business, underpriced their policies to be more competitive. They were working on the assumption that, as with life insurance policies that consumers routinely drop after a few years, many consumers would allow their LTC policies to lapse over time. Insurers would keep the premiums that had already been paid and apply that money to claims filed by those who kept their policies. Only the insurers misjudged the popularity of LTC contracts among those who bought them. LTC benefits proved wildly more popular than insurers anticipated, and lapse rates were exceedingly small. Insurers were unprepared to cover the resulting claims and requested that state insurance commissions allow for rate increases to cover the insurers' spiraling costs.

Today, such problems are, for the most part, in the past. Stronger insurers have absorbed the weaker LTC underwriters, and mispriced policies are less common. However, rate increases can—and do—still occur. To protect yourself as well as possible, stick to the highest-rated insurance companies (see my note about Moody's and Standard & Poor's in the section on annuities). Moreover, to lessen the risk that you will one day be slapped with a rate increase, look to insurers who have been active in the industry for years and never raised rates on policyholders. One telling sign that an insurer is properly pricing policies: It pays a dividend on its LTC contracts. Most don't; a small handful, including New York Life and Northwestern Mutual, do. The dividend is an indication that the company is taking in an appropriate amount of premium to cover its claims, and is then returning excess premium to its policyholders. The added benefit of the dividend, of course, is that it serves to effectively lower your annual premium.

Finally, the best long-term care policies will include a nonforfeiture clause that can protect you to a certain degree from premiums that rise beyond your reach. In that event, a nonforfeiture clause will require the insurer to pay daily costs up to the amount of premium you paid in over the years, though don't expect inflation protection. If you've paid $20,000 in premiums over, say, ten years before a rate increase makes the policy unaffordable, then your insurer must pay $20,000 worth of daily costs.

22

Pillow Talk—Who's Really in Charge, Financially?

When I was young, there were few married women in the workforce. In the traditional family of that day, the husband had the role of family provider—in rural America, he plowed the fields, harvested the crops, and gathered the family's meager income. The wives cared for the children, kept the house, washed the clothes, cooked the meals. In rural America, the wife fed the domestic livestock, gathered eggs, milked cows, churned butter, tended the family garden, then canned the family fruit and produce, and, of course, cooked, cleaned, washed, and sewed.

World War II changed all that. The men went to war. The wives were left in complete charge of the family—including family finances. In order to supplement the meager allotments from their military husbands, many women entered the workforce—especially in the rapidly growing defense industries.

Things were never the same after the war. Women enjoyed their newfound roles and their release from drudgery. Some sixty years after the end of World War II, women are educated as lawyers and doctors and educators and physicists. Some are highly paid corporate executives. Some have founded lucrative businesses. A number are judges, governors, senators, congressmen, and mayors.

These highly compensated women will never be content to be paid a household allowance by a breadwinner husband who controls the family finances. As the saying goes, "You've come a long way, baby." Indeed she has. The old way will not return in our lifetime or ever!

Still, in our modern world there are women who are pleased to be sheltered wives and mothers who really do not want any part of the corporate rat race, nor do they bother to learn about finances. When they are divorced, or when they are widowed, they feel helpless and unable to cope with the complexities of modern financial life. How much worse if they lack financial job skills, yet have the obligation of raising one or more little children?

In truth, the fastest-growing segment of poor in America is composed of single women with children (divorced, widowed, or with children born out of wedlock).

It is absolutely mandatory that every married woman understand the family finances, extent of savings, debt obligations, insurance coverage, and tax liability. Wives must understand that they are personally liable for taxes and penalties or claims of fraud for joint tax returns that they sign with their spouses. Don't sign any legal document that you don't understand!

Wives must prepare themselves for the time when they become widows or divorcees. For men and women, there is no better investment than an investment in job training or the acquisition of new skills. In a turbulent employment market, if one set of skills is no longer in demand, there may well be openings for the other skills that you have learned. There is now available a plethora of courses online dealing with every phase of finance. I would particularly urge everyone to consider a course in business law. In today's bad times, literally thousands of men and women are losing their jobs. They become desolate—even suicidal. The best answer to your problem is simple. Your employer is not your source. The federal or state government is not your source. God is your source. He has all wealth and is abundantly able to care for those that are His. I laughingly say, "God's petty cash fund is greater than all the debts of the United States government." If you learn to trust Him, He can and will show you avenues of financial provision of which you may never have dreamed.

Let me illustrate. At CBN, we had a volunteer female weekend receptionist whose extreme overweight had brought on crippling arthritis. One Sunday evening as I returned from an out of town trip, she called out to me, sobbing, "Oh, Pat, what am I going to do? I have no income and my welfare has been cut off!"

She had not learned that welfare was not her source. God was her source. So I asked her, "Don't you have any skills that you could use to earn money?"

"I can make Christmas ornaments," she replied. Well, she could indeed. She was a gifted crafter. She could take the hollowed frames of empty cat food cans, wrap them in beautiful ribbon, place inside of their frame charming manger scenes, and then secure them with a small red ribbon to hang on a Christmas tree. The effect was exquisite. She would also take empty egg shells and place within them lovely tiny Christmas scenes. I told her that I would help her place these ornaments for sale in various religious supply stores in the local area. I would have gladly given her modest financial backing, but such backing never became necessary. I saw her several months later and asked how her business was doing. "Oh," she said, "business is so good that I have hired four people to help with the work!"

You see, the Virginia Welfare Department was not this woman's source. God was her source, and in her trouble provided her with more than she could have imagined. She just had to employ the God-given talent that had been hers all along. So ask yourself: What are the marketable skills God has given me? The answer will amaze you.

Back to the financial roles of husbands and wives in marriage. Ongoing strife over finances is either the first or second leading cause of divorce in America—profligate husbands or profligate wives on the one hand, or tight-fisted men and up-tight women on the other.

I once knew a freewheeling Texas businessman whose glamorous wife was constantly overdrawing her bank account, to his acute embarrassment. When confronted with the problem, this self-indulgent lady smiled sweetly and said, "I'm not overdrawn, I'm underdeposited."

In another case, the wife brought the family near bankruptcy by wild shopping binges, charging tens of thousands of dollars' of jewelry and expensive clothes for which her husband was forced to deplete his savings to pay.

On the other side of the ledger is the tight-fisted tyrant who has control of all the family money regardless of the source and demands, under penalty of an abusive rage, a detailed accounting of every penny his wife spends.

Granted, these are extreme cases, but they occur all too often in real life. Every wife was once a little girl and then a teenager. She may have been brought up with a healthy understanding of money and its use and abuse; or she may have been the spoiled princess of overindulgent parents who never denied her anything; or she may have been brought up in a family that constantly struggled financially, in which frugality or fear was the norm.

Those coming up from poverty can either hoard every dollar or can, on the other hand, be so determined never to be poor again that they become obsessed and ruthless to acquire great wealth and the trappings of a conspicuous lifestyle.

Many parents demonstrate before their children a healthy attitude toward money. They live within their means. They pay the bills on time. They give and they save. Children brought up in such surroundings will naturally take on the habits they observe in their parents, especially if they have been taught by their parents to live within an allowance, to give, to save, and to invest. Even better if they learn that extra purchases must be paid for from the proceeds of a summer job or a paper route or lawn care service.

Real work is wonderful financial training for school-age children. The summer I turned thirteen, my father sent me to work at the large farm of a distant relative. I was paid fifteen dollars a month plus room and board. My day started at 5:30 A.M. and during harvest would end at 8:00 or 9:00 P.M. I stacked shocks of wheat and oats, ricked itchy straw in front of a blower from a threshing machine, pitched hay, mowed pastures behind a team of mules, hauled heavy sacks of potatoes, chopped wood, cleared underbrush, and did it all under a blazing sun. The lessons I learned were invaluable. More than anything, I was trained to do hard work. The meager pay was secondary, but I certainly learned the value of each hard-earned dollar. This summer was wonderful preparation for my later life. Which is better—my experience or the experience of the overindulged, overweight teenager of today absorbed in rock music and video games?

Before marriage, a prospective husband and wife should spend time learning about each other's experience and attitude toward money. Does the prospective mate know or even care about hard work and financial management? Is the prospective mate a formerly self-indulged child, unable to deny himself anything regardless of cost? Is there a mommy or daddy in the background who shields the grown child from financial reality and responsibility? A prospective spouse should never allow himself or herself to be deluded into thinking "after we are married I can change him (or her)." It won't happen. Why take on a lifetime of struggle, angry recriminations, and financial peril? Move on. With six billion people in the world, surely there is someone you can find who is more suitable for you.

But what if you are already married? I believe that God can change people. If a husband and wife sincerely submit themselves to God's will for their marriage, He will show them how to fix their financial problems. First, pray about the problem. Then talk frankly and openly about finances without accusations, anger, or tears. What is needed is calm common sense, and possibly the help of an expert financial planner.

Sometimes one spouse is skillful in recordkeeping, budgeting, and bill paying. There are instances when highly compensated husbands cannot control their personal spending. In that case, they agree to accept a modest cash allowance for personal expenses (with no credit cards). Their wives handle everything else. In other cases, it falls to the husband to handle all the financial details, and the wife has an allowance and a checking account for household expenses and her personal needs.

When husband and wife each are earning income, they can agree to pool their income and spend and invest according to an agreed-upon budget.

But I believe that a better plan is for the husband to have his own bank and brokerage account and for the wife to have her bank and brokerage account. They can then agree on which expenses are whose responsibility.

In some measure, this will depend on which income is the greatest. If, say, the husband has the largest income, the couple could agree that he would pay their mortgage payments on the house, the insurance payments, medical costs, the car payments, major repairs, as well as his personal expenses. The wife could pay school fees, the children's clothes, her clothes and personal care, the family groceries, club dues, her transportation, babysitters, and domestic help, if any. They could agree on which party pays agreed-upon charitable contributions. Income taxes on a joint return should be paid by each spouse according to the tax liability that their respective income generates. Also consider the costs of family vacations, trips, and so on. I think it is a splendid idea for a working wife to have her own 401(k) plan at work and any other investments that she can generate.

Lest there begin selfish bickering over who owns what, the couple should clearly and prayerfully decide on their priorities and life goals. And then they must agree on a family budget. They are partners together in life with the Lord as their head. If two people truly love God and love each other, they can build a satisfying life together, and their family finances can grow dramatically by their mutual efforts. On the other hand, the clear warning of Jesus Christ is as true today as it was the day it was uttered: "A house divided against itself cannot stand."

23

A Business of Your Own

I recently was astounded as I leafed through the Verizon telephone yellow pages covering the combined communities where I live along with 1.5 million other people. There were over 1,700 pages filled with listings ranging from abortion alternatives through kennels and pet grooming to woodworking and X-ray imaging. There were thousands and thousands of small businesses and professional people seeking to serve a discreet niche in our relatively modest metropolitan area. I thought this is the essence of the free enterprise system which has brought our nation such incredible prosperity—not government, not giant industrial combines—simply thousands of Americans offering their unique skills for a profit to meet the specific needs of their fellow citizens.

The American system is unique because of the ease of entry our laws provide to prospective entrepreneurs. In some societies, the government considers a new business a threat either to the established order or to the power of the government itself. In restrictive societies, someone who wants to open a retail stand to sell fruit or vegetables is faced with months or even years of bureaucratic red tape and complex licensing.

In the United States, a person is free to pursue his or her dream. Free to succeed—free to fail. Sometimes only a simple inexpensive business license is required. Many times nothing is required but the skill, the creativity, and perseverance of the entrepreneur.

Although publicity is usually directed toward the industrial giants like IBM, Alcoa, General Motors, or General Electric, in truth the great corporations account for only twenty percent of the job creation in this country. Eighty percent of the jobs are created by the tens of thousands of businesses that employ less than 200 workers each.

Small business is good for the country. Economic freedom brings prosperity and a better way of life. Monopoly and excessive bureaucratic regulation stifle individual initiative and will ultimately send even the most prosperous nations into economic decline.

Any entrepreneur has freedom to work or not to work, to buy and to sell at the prices and profits a free market allows. An entrepreneur may, in a nondiscriminatory way, hire whomever he or she wants…locate where he or she wants…expand the business as his best judgment directs. He no longer has to accede to the wishes of a "boss." He or she is the "boss." For the entrepreneur, the sky is the limit and the reward of his labors belongs ultimately to him, not the distant shareholders of an impersonal corporation.

That's the good side. The down side risks are substantial. Until the business is established, there are no regular pay checks. In fact, a truly successful start-up entrepreneur will initially take no money for himself out of the business. The nine to five work day is a thing of the past. So are health benefits, guaranteed retirement, and generous expense accounts.

The start-up entrepreneur is responsible for books and records, tax filings, sales and marketing, product development, payables, receivables, payrolls, real estate, and banking. For success it takes undivided effort, hard work, and long hours. In the early days it takes the sacrifice of family time and fun time.

For married couples, it takes the wholehearted agreement—and hopefully the participation—of both spouses. It takes prayer and a willingness to sacrifice immediate gratification for long range freedom and prosperity.

Actually, starting a business is not as hard as it sounds, and there are many along the way that want to help you succeed.

Let me give a few examples. In the Philippines, outside the capital Manila, is a huge garbage dump call Payatas. It is a stinking, loathsome place, but it serves as a home for some wretched people who make a living from the garbage. One individual living there was contacted by a seller of used shoes to find for him the uppers of discarded shoes. After a while, the poverty-stricken man determined that he could rehab the shoes himself at a profit. All he needed was "capital" to buy the supplies to get started. Our ministry was helping these people to have a better life, and we were only too happy to advance to the budding entrepreneur the "capital" he needed—the princely sum of twenty U.S. dollars. In a short time, he was selling three pairs of shoes a week, had lifted himself and his family out of poverty, and was on the way to business success.

Two years ago, one of my granddaughters went on a mission trip to Thailand where she visited a struggling orphanage. The orphans were able to craft attractive shoulder bags for ladies. My granddaughter promptly named these accessories "Thai-Totes," and showed them to several high-end women's apparel stores which agreed to purchase these inexpensive items. They quickly sold out at a price of $50 apiece. The substantial profits were then sent to the orphanage for its expenses and the purchase of new supplies for "Thai-Totes."

On a larger scale is the story of an MBA graduate from Regent University who learned that many of the nation's clothing manufacturers had large stocks of garments which they had not sold. He made arrangements to take the most desirable items on consignment, and then sell them at bargain prices on eBay. Within a couple of years, his gross sales were $100 million and he had become the number one merchandiser on that popular website.

It all starts with an idea. What need exists in your community or in the nation that you could fill? What is your passion? What skill do you have which might have commercial possibilities?

Next you need to perform some simple market tests. Who else is doing what you want to do and how well do they do it? If you produce something, will anyone be interested in buying it? What price can you get and is it possible to produce the product or service profitably, taking into account all of the costs associated? Can you find a product (and there are thousands of them) for which you could be an independent sales representative? If so, could you possibly sell it over the telephone or over the Internet from your home? Many housewives have found extremely lucrative sales opportunities in real estate. It is necessary to pass an examination, but beyond that you can set your own schedule depending on how much income you would like to make.

In general, business is usually conducted in one of three forms—a sole proprietorship, a partnership, or a stock corporation.

If you decide to open a bakery and own it and run it yourself, you are the sole proprietor. You can have a joint ownership agreement with your spouse, but, absent a clear partnership agreement, this is still a proprietorship... for example, "Acme Bakers, Joe and Jane Smith, Proprietors."

For tax purposes, profits of a proprietorship are considered as ordinary income to you (or to you and your spouse) and business losses can be deducted from your other ordinary income. In other words, your business is an extension of yourself. You must pay double social security taxes (self employer/employee employment taxes) on earnings up to the federal social security cut-off.

The danger of a sole proprietorship is your exposure to lawsuits. If a patron is injured, you are personally liable. If an employee has a grievance, your bank account, your home, your stocks and bonds are all at risk. You can carry insurance, but your insurance may prove inadequate or monthly insurance costs may become a costly drain on your income.

Few people today should choose to do business as a partnership. Partnerships have few tax advantages and over the years reveal an unexpected complexity that can lead to serious trouble. However, there are so-called "Master Limited Partnerships" for certain projects like oil and gas pipelines. Certain real estate and natural resource businesses are conducted as partnerships with the general partner running the business (and taking the risks) while the "limited partners" customarily have no obligation other than the money they have agreed to pay into the venture.

For the fledgling entrepreneur, I strongly urge a simple stock corporation. A corporation can be organized with as little as $1,000 in capital and with yourself as sole director. There are simple forms that can be used for the Articles of Incorporation and the Bylaws of a corporation. You can incorporate in any state, but a state with no corporate income tax (such as Nevada) is preferable. Call the office of the Secretary of State and ask for the required forms and costs. Send to the Secretary of State the Articles of Incorporation that you have drafted naming the corporation, its purposes, its director or directors, along with a couple of checks that total about $35, plus the name of some resident such as the C.T. Corporation who is authorized to receive process on behalf of the corporation. In about a week, you will receive your official Certificate of Incorporation. Then you buy what is called a "corporate outfit"—a stock record book, blank shares with the name of the corporation, an official seal, and a journal for keeping the minutes of shareholder meetings and directors meetings.

At the first meeting, you issue yourself 1,000 shares with a par value of $0.01, pay $100 or $1,000 into the corporate treasury, declare an official shareholders meeting, elect yourself sole director, then pass a resolution to open a bank account, adopt the bylaws, and, if you wish, elect yourself, your spouse, and/or your children corporate officers.

It is that simple. From then on, you can do business as a corporation in whatever legal way you see fit.

Within a couple of weeks, your corporation would be advised

to mail to the IRS a simple form stating that it chooses a "Sub S" election. This means that the corporation will owe no federal income taxes. As a Sub Chapter S Corporation, its losses and gains will be apportioned to its shareholder or shareholders.

I strongly advise you to keep very good records and to hold regular meetings of shareholders and directors. It may seem strange to have meetings with yourself, but the formal record is important. The corporation gives you shelter from civil lawsuits so long as it clearly is used as a business and is not merely an alter ego to you. In lawsuits, judges are very reluctant to "pierce the corporate veil" and allow legal action against the shareholders of a corporation. That is why it is necessary to observe the necessary formalities to prove that the corporation has a life of its own.

Of course, as you grow, it is a very simple matter to add more directors and to sell stock to other investors. One technique that I have used is to have "A" and "B" shares. By a simple vote of the shareholders (you), there can be created two classes of stock—one having multiple votes per share and one having one vote. Both can share equally in dividend and distributions, but the multiple vote shares control the Board of Directors of the corporation, and thereby its future direction.

If you are the sole shareholder, the affairs of your corporation can be quite simple. Shareholders can split the shares as they see fit, add new shares, issue preferred shares, issue preferred shares or debentures that can be converted into common stock, and grant employee stock options. Either at inception or as the levels of complexity increase, it is advisable to have the advice either of a tax specialist or a modestly priced corporate lawyer.

I have noticed one noted trial lawyer advertising a website called LegalZoom.com that offers the nuts and bolts of corporate organization at what appears to be a very modest fee.

In addition to modest protection from lawsuits, the corporate form of business has several important advantages. The tax code normally allows tax deductions for expenses incurred in the pursuit of business profit. A corporation by its very nature normally overcomes that hurdle. Legitimate deductions for payroll, depreciation, rent, utilities, supplies, etc., are not routinely challenged. For instance, if you employ your child as a corporate maintenance man or sales person, their salary or commissions should be a deductible corporate expense. The possibility of a challenge in the same situation if you are a sole proprietor is much higher. There is also less hassle over the tax write-offs provided for new equipment, use of a vehicle, rental of a home office, etc.

An interesting sidelight of the tax code was introduced by the late Senator John Sherman Cooper of Kentucky. For those who would like to turn their interest in horses into a business, the law is clear. The enterprise must have all of the attributes of a profit-making enterprise (not a hobby) and must show a profit in at least two out of seven years. The costs of maintaining these animals are deductible and their purchase price may be written off against ordinary income in either three, five, or seven years.

For those who like farming, gardening, or animal husbandry, there are remarkable profit potentials. About twenty years ago, I had a fabulous steak dinner at the home of an animal farmer in central Iowa. He had an office with a computer geared to the grain and meat prices at the Chicago Board of Trade. As we looked at his prize animals and discussed the price of farm acreage and the protein content of his feed, he made this amazing statement about the various federal subsidies available to small farmers, "I give more attention to farming the government programs than I do to farming the land."

The Federal government has long been the farmers' friend. I would strongly advise anyone interested in agriculture to contact your resident agricultural agent to learn of the intellectual assistance, the soil and seed research, the crop studies, forestry, the agricultural loan programs, and the direct grants available to farmers of all types and sizes…whether organized as proprietor-ships or cooperatives or corporations. Some opportunities in this field may amaze you.

For your business, I would suggest a simple computer accounting system called "QuickBooks" that will do most of the accounting calculations a business requires. To take advantage of the remarkable numbers of tax deductions available to you, I strongly recommend consulting a tax professional who can give you tips on tax advantages, strategies, and who will prepare your annual tax return.

Some are thinking, "I just can't do it. It's too complicated." No, it's not. At its heart, business involves selling something that someone else wants at a price greater than what it costs you. Anyone who can do third grade arithmetic can be in business. Whether man or woman, do not be intimidated. Business is common sense. You provide something that is useful or desirable for someone else. You sell it at what it costs to replace, plus a share of overhead expenses, plus a profit to take care of your needs with something to reinvest and grow. An MBA from Harvard is not necessary. Some of the most successful people of wealth in the world have no formal education. They do have, however, an indomitable spirit and the will to win.

During the giddy days of what is called the "Dot Com" boom, young entrepreneurs clamored to do an IPO (Initial Public Offering). The lure was irresistible. Shares of start-up companies with no earnings, little or no capital, and armed with a one-page pie-in-the-sky power point presentation were offered to the public at insane valuations. A partner in one of the largest Silicon Valley investment houses boasted to me that some of their start-up companies had price earning multiples that looked like ZIP codes.

A corporation is normally valued (priced) in some relationship to its Price Earnings Ratio (P.E.). That is the price of a share of the stock divided by its share of the corporation's earnings. Other metrics of valuation are its price to sales; or to its price to assets; or to its price to so-called EBITDA, which is the earnings before deductions for interest expense, taxes, depreciation, and amortization.

In a normal world (*which excludes the current recession*), the value of your business on a public market would be approximately ten times its earnings, or two to three times its sales, or six to eight times its EBITDA, or, depending on the business, 1.5 to 2.5 times its book value. Another measure is the Price Earnings divided by the growth rate of earnings, or PEG ratio.

Assume that your business has grown so that its annual gross sales are $5,000,000. That could mean a value of $10,000,000 to $15,000,000. If the earnings are $1,000,000, the value could be $10,000,000 or, depending on its growth rate, $20,000,000. If the EBITDA is $1,500,000, then the value would be between $9,000,000 and $12,000,000.

Each share of the company would have a market value based on its percentage ownership of the total value of the company. Assuming one million shares and no debt, then each share would have a paper value somewhere between $10 and $20. What could change this would be the corporation's development of a breakthrough patent or process that would have such an economic potential that the pricing would be based on a much higher so-called "forward P.E." (Of course, the stock market would have to be willing to accept this accelerated valuation.)

Accessing the public markets provides the owner or owners of a business a reliable indicator of the value of their holdings plus a measure of liquidity if they wish to dispose of all or a portion of their holdings.

About ten to fifteen years ago, a public offering of the stock in a corporation was relatively simple and inexpensive. Small companies could list on the so-called "pink sheets"; large companies could list on the electronic NASDAQ; and those desiring more traditional listings could choose either the New York Stock Exchange or the smaller American Stock Exchange.

However, the Congress has erected a hurdle to public listing called Sarbanes-Oxley. This law requires auditing and compliance that could cost a small company up to $300,000 per year, plus it exacts criminal penalties on the corporate CEO if he signs a reporting document that is inaccurate, whether or not he was aware of the error. This law has had the effect of killing access to public capital for small companies, but Congress may become aware of its error and fix it.

In summary, I cannot emphasize strongly enough the tremendous benefits of owning your own business in whatever form it takes. Sure there are difficulties, but in a free country the field is always wide open and the opportunities available to you are unlimited.

Conclusion

In conclusion, our economy has encountered one of the worst periods in its history. The global economy is experiencing shockwaves that can only be experienced every hundred years or so.

Keep in mind that bad times have taken place in the past, and they undoubtedly will take place in the future. As bad as the Great Depression was in 1929, 1930, 1931, and 1932, even though unemployment hit 25 percent, there were still 75 percent of the people who were employed. Even though the stock market hit historic lows in the early thirties, the gains from those lows were disproportionately great. The foundations of great fortunes were laid by astute investors who found underpriced diamonds in the midst of the wreckage.

Above all else, remember that God is Almighty and He is greater than any business downturn. He knows who you are. He knows where you are. And He understands even greater than you do what your needs are. He will not leave you nor forsake you. So take heart, and look for the opportunities that are all around you.

Glossary

adjustable-rate mortgage (ARM). Mortgage loan that allows the interest rate to be changed at specific intervals over the maturity of the loan.

american depositary shares. Underlying shares of American Depositary Receipts (ADRs), which are receipts issued by U.S. banks to domestic buyers as a convenient substitute for direct ownership of stock in foreign companies.

annuity. Contract sold by commercial insurance companies that pays a monthly (or quarterly, semiannual, or annual) income benefit for the life of a person, for the lives of two or more persons, or for a specified period of time.

asset allocation. Method of targeting investments to allocate proportions of asset classes to achieve the highest investment return while minimizing risk.

balance sheet. Financial statement that gives an accounting picture of property owned by a company or an individual and of claims against the property on a specific date; a snapshot of the financial position of an individual or company at one point in time.

blue chip. Common stock or a nationally known company that has a long record of profit growth and dividend payment and a reputation for quality management, products and services.

bric countries refers to the rapidly developing group of countries that are Brazil, Russia, India, and China. The term was first used in a thesis written by Jim O'Neill, a global economist at Goldman Sachs.

brokerage account. Customer account at a brokerage. There are three kinds of brokerage accounts—cash-management, margin, and discretionary.

call, also known as a Call Option. The right, purchased by an investor, to buy a certain number of shares of a particular stock or stock index at a predetermined price before a preset deadline.

callable bonds. Bonds that are redeemable by the issuer before the scheduled maturity date; usually called when interest rates fall so significantly that the issuer can save money by issuing new bonds at lower rates.

capital appreciation. Increase in value over time of money or other property owned.

capital gain. Gain on the sale of a capital asset (property held for investment).

cash-out refinancing. Mortgage refinancing transaction in which the new mortgage amount is greater than the existing mortgage amount, plus loan settlement costs. The purpose of a cash-out refinance is to extract equity from the borrower's home.

certificate of deposit (CD). Debt instrument issued by a bank that usually pays interest. Maturities range from a few weeks to several years.

closed-end investment fund. Investment company that operates a mutual fund with a limited number of shares.

collateralized debt obligation (CDO). Sophisticated financial tool that repackages individual loans into a product that can be sold on the secondary market. These packages consist of auto loans, credit card debt, mortgages, or corporate debt. They are called collateralized because they have some type of collateral behind them.

commission. Fee paid to an employee or agent for services performed, especially a percentage of a total amount received in a transaction.

commodity. A tangible good; bulk goods such as grains, metals, and foods are tracked on a commodities exchange.

common stock. Security representing an ownership interest (equity) in a corporation.

compound interest. Interest earned on principal plus interest that was earned earlier; interest can be compounded on a daily, quarterly, annual, or other basis.

comprehensive and collision insurance. Optional types of auto insurance that protect your car if it is damaged. Comprehensive insurance covers damage to your car if it is stolen; or damaged by flood, fire, or animals. Collision covers damage to your car when your car hits, or is hit by, another vehicle, or other object.

credit default swap. Designed to transfer the credit exposure of fixed income products between parties; essentially an insurance policy against default. The buyer of a credit swap receives credit protection, whereas the seller of the swap guarantees the credit worthiness of the product. By doing this, the risk of default is transferred from the holder of the fixed income security to the seller of the swap.

credit-counseling agency. Credit advisory service offered to persons with excessive debts as an alternative to bankruptcy. Debt counselors affiliated with the National Foundation for Consumer Credit charge only a nominal monthly fee for helping consumers work their way out of debt. Consumers are budgeted a portion of take-home income to pay off current obligations and voluntarily curb their use of credit until debts are repaid.

credit report. An account of your credit history, prepared by a credit bureau. A credit report will contain both credit history, such as what you owe to whom and whether you make the payments on time, as well as personal history, such as your former addresses, employment record, and lawsuits in which you have been involved. An estimated 50 percent of all credit reports contain errors, such as accounts that don't belong to you, an incorrect account status or information reported that is older than seven years (ten years in the case of a bankruptcy).

credit score. Measure of borrower credit risk commonly used by creditors, including mortgage loan originators; some factors used to determine include income, assets, length of employment, length living in one place, and past record of using credit.

currency-trading account. An account set up to exchange one currency for another; for example, U.S. dollars for euros. Currencies trade in pairs and a trader buys the currency that he thinks will appreciate in value relative to the other.

default risk. Measurable possibility of a debtor's failure to make timely payments of interest and principal as they come due or to meet some other provision of a bond, mortgage, lease, or other contract

deflation. Decline in the prices of goods and services; the reverse of inflation.

depression. Economic condition characterized by a massive decrease in business activity, falling prices, reduced purchasing power, an excess of supply over demand, rising unemployment, accumulating inventories, deflation, plant contraction, public fear, and caution.

derivative. Security taking its value from another security, asset, or index; collateralized debt obligations, options, or futures would be examples.

discretionary income. Spendable income remaining after the purchase of physical necessities, such as food, clothing, and shelter, as well as the payment of taxes.

diversified portfolio. Group of securities held by an individual or institutional investor which contain appropriate selections from the equity, capital, and money markets in an effort to reduce overall risk.

dividend. Payment by a corporation to shareholders, generally taxable as ordinary income.

Dow Jones Industrial Average. The most widely followed benchmark of stock market performance, containing value changes for thirty large corporations.

emerging market. Used to describe a nation's social or business activity in the process of rapid growth and industrialization.

exchange-traded fund (ETF). Securities that closely resemble index funds, but can be bought and sold during the day just like common stocks. These investment vehicles allow investors a convenient way to purchase a broad basket of securities in a single transaction. Essentially, ETFs offer the convenience of a stock along with the diversification of a mutual fund.

exercise price. Amount at which a put or call can be used to buy a stock, or a convertible security can be redeemed for shares of stock.

exponential curve. Technical name for the curve that results from graphing the periodic values of an investment with compounding interest.

fed discount window. The Federal Reserve can loan money to banks at the discount rate to make sure they can meet the reserve requirement when they close each night. This tool is called the Fed's use of credit, or discount window.

federal deposit insurance corporation (FDIC). Independent federal agency, established in 1933, that insures deposits up to $100,000 in member commercial banks.

federal reserve board. Governing board of the Federal Reserve System, which establishes policies on bank regulations, rates at which banks can borrow (discount rate), and how much available credit is in the market among other things.

financial statements. Written records of the financial status of an individual, association, or business organization; typically includes a balance sheet, an income statement, and a statement of cash flows.

529 College Savings Plan, also known as the Qualified Tuition Program. An investment vehicle created under the Small Business Job Protection Act of 1996 that allows individuals to make tax-deductible contributions to accounts that accumulate tax-free income if used to cover a beneficiary's qualified educational expenses.

fixed annuity. Investment contract sold by an insurance company that guarantees fixed payments, either for life or for a specified period.

fixed-rate mortgage. Type of mortgage in which the interest rate does not fluctuate with general market conditions.

401(k) retirement-savings plan. Plan that allows an employee to contribute pretax earnings to a company pool, which is invested in stocks, bonds, or money market instruments.

frontier markets. Small, illiquid stock markets that are generally considered to be at a much earlier stage of economic and financial market development than emerging markets.

futures contract. Agreement to buy or sell a specific amount of a commodity or financial instrument at a particular price on a stipulated future date.

guaranteed return. Generated by contract between an institution and an investor that guarantees a minimum or specific rate of return on the invested capital over the life of the contract.

high-yield bond. Bond with a speculative credit rating of BB or lower by Standard & Poor's and Moody's ratings; typically issued by companies without long track records or with questionable credit strength.

immediate annuity makes income payments immediately, or very soon after purchase. You use an immediate annuity when you want to start taking income as soon as possible.

index annuity. A fixed annuity, either immediate or deferred, that earns interest or provides benefits that are linked to an external equity reference or an equity index.

index fund. Mutual fund whose portfolio matches that of a broad-based index such as Standard & Poor's or that of a broad-based sector of the economy and whose performance therefore mirrors the market as a whole or a sector as a whole.

individual retirement account (IRA). Trust fund to which any individual employee can contribute up to the allowable amount per year, depending on your level of income and participation in another qualified retirement plan your contribution may be tax-deductible.

inflation. Rise in the prices of goods and services, as happens when spending increases faster than the supply of goods on the market.

interest payment. Actual cost of using credit or another's money.

interest rate. Cost of using money, expressed as a rate per period of time, usually one year, in which case it is called annual rate of interest.

investing. Transferring capital to an enterprise in order to secure income or profit for the investor.

investment account. Contractual relationship between financial institution and investor for the purposes of purchasing stocks, bonds, mutual fund shares, real property, or other assets with the expectation of obtaining income or capital gain—or both—in the future.

investment-grade bond. Term used to describe bonds suitable for purchase by prudent investors.

laddering. Purchasing CDs or bonds that mature at various intervals to provide greater access to cash or greater regularity of income and protection against interest rate fluctuations.

liability insurance. Protection from claims arising from injuries or damage to other people or property.

long-term care insurance. Contract to cover day-to-day care that a patient receives in a nursing facility or in his/her residence following an illness or injury, or in old age in return for premiums.

market risk, also known as Systematic Risk. Risk inherent in a security that cannot be diversified away.

maturity. Date at which legal rights in something ripen; time at which an action can enforce payment.

medicaid. Jointly administered federal and state government health insurance for people who have low income and limited assets.

medicare. Federal health insurance program that covers people who are sixty-five or older, people of any age with permanent kidney failure, and those under sixty-five who have been receiving Social Security disability benefits for the past twenty-four months.

minimum balance for credit cards, also known as Minimum Payment, is minimum amount that a consumer is required to pay on a revolving charge account in order to keep the account in good standing. For checking, savings, and other accounts it is the minimum amount required to start and/or to be kept in an account.

m1 money supply. The sum of currency, demand deposits (checking, NOW accounts), travelers' checks, etc.

monetary policy. The efforts of a nation's central bank aimed at influencing inflation rates, economic growth, and interest rates by varying the supply of money.

money market account. Special savings-account which pays fluctuating interest rate that, on average, is higher than the interest rate on ordinary savings accounts.

money-market fund. Open-ended mutual fund that invests in commercial paper, bankers' acceptances, repurchase agreements, government securities, certificates of deposit, and other highly liquid and safe securities.

mortgage-backed security. Security backed by a mortgage on real estate.

mutual fund. A type of regulated investment company that raises money from shareholders and invests it in stocks, bonds, options, commodities, or money market securities.

net asset value (NAV). Accounting term used in reference to the value of mutual fund and similar investment shares.

net present value. Method of determining whether the expected financial performance of a proposed investment promises to be adequate.

option. The right, but not obligation, to buy or sell property that is granted in exchange for an agreed-upon sum.

par value. Stated or face value of a stock or bond. It has little significance for common stock but on bonds it specifies the payment at maturity.

permanent insurance, also known as Whole Life Insurance. Policy that offers protection in case the insured dies and also builds up cash surrender value at a guaranteed rate, which can be borrowed against.

point for real estate is upfront fee charged by lender, designed to decrease the overall rate the borrower pays. One point is equal to 1 percent.

preferred stock. Part of the capital stock of a corporation that enjoys priority over the remaining or common stock in the distribution of dividends and in the event of dissolution of the corporation, also in the distribution of assets.

purchasing power. Value of money as measured by the goods and services it can buy.

put, also known as a Put Option. Contract that grants the right to sell at a specified price a specific number of shares by a certain date.

real estate investment trust (REIT). A real estate mutual fund, allowed by income tax laws to avoid the corporate income tax; it sells shares of ownership and must invest in real estate or mortgages.

recession. Downturn in economic activity, defined by many economists as at least two consecutive quarters of decline in a country's Gross Domestic Product (or final value of goods and services produced in a national economy).

risk-free rate of return. The interest rate on the safest investments, such as federal government obligations.

risk tolerance. An investor's ability to handle declines in the value of his or her portfolio of investments.

Roth IRA. Permits account holders to allow their capital to accumulate tax free under certain conditions, named after Delaware Senator William V. Roth, Jr.

S&P 500, also known as Standard & Poor's Index. Broad-based measurement of changes in stock market conditions based on the average performance of 500 widely held common stocks.

SEP IRA, also known as Simplified Employee Pension Plan. Retirement plan specifically designed for self-employed people and small business owners.

securities. Stock certificates, bonds, and other evidence of a secured indebtedness or of a right created in the holder to participate in the profits or assets distribution of a profit-making enterprise.

securities and exchange commission (SEC). Federal agency empowered to regulate and supervise the selling of securities, to prevent unfair practices on security exchanges and over-the-counter markets, and to maintain a fair and orderly market for the investor.

Social Security, technically known as the Social Security Act. Federal retirement plan enacted by Congress in 1935 to require the current working generation to contribute to the support of older, retired workers.

split-adjusted price. Price of a stock after its number of shares outstanding is increased to make the stock more marketable; the total value of a stock remains unchanged after a split. For example, if you owned ten shares at $1 (value of $10) before a two-for-one split, you would own twenty shares at $0.50 (value of $10) afterwards.

stagflation. Term coined by economists in the 1970s to describe the previously unprecedented combination of slow economic growth and high unemployment (stagnation) with rising prices (inflation).

stock market. Organized market, such as a stock exchange or an over-the-counter market, where stocks and bonds are actively traded.

taxable income. Any amount of income subject to income tax; various deductions to gross income exist for individuals and businesses bringing taxable income down in many instances.

tax-equivalent yield. Pretax yield that a taxable bond would have to pay to equal the tax-free yield of a municipal bond in an investor's tax bracket.

term insurance. Coverage that stays in effect for only a specified, limited period. If the insured dies within that period, the beneficiary receives the death payments otherwise the policy ends and the beneficiary receives nothing.

treasuries. Negotiable debt obligations of the U.S. government secured by its full faith and credit and issued at various schedules and maturities; includes Treasury bills, Treasury bonds, and Treasury notes.

variable annuity. Life insurance annuity whose value fluctuates with that of an underlying securities portfolio or other index of performance.

variable rate mortgage. See adjustable-rate mortgage.

volatility measures size and frequency of fluctuations in the price of a particular stock, bond, or commodity.

wall street analyst, also called sell-side analyst. Investment community research analyst employed by a brokerage firm or another firm that manages client accounts.

yield. Return on an investor's capital investment. For bonds it is the coupon rate of interest divided by the purchase price (also known as current yield). For stocks it is the percentage rate of return paid on a common or preferred stock in dividends.

yield-to-call. Yield on a bond assuming the bond will be redeemed by the issuer at the first call date specified in the indenture agreement.

yield-to-maturity. Calculation of yield on a bond, from the current date until it is scheduled to be retired, that takes into account the capital gain on a discount bond or capital loss on a premium bond.

Index

About the Author

M. G. "Pat" Robertson has achieved national and international recognition as a religious broadcaster, philanthropist, educator, religious leader, businessman, and author. He is the founder and chairman of The Christian Broadcasting Network (CBN) Inc., and founder of International Family Entertainment Inc., Regent University, Operation Blessing International Relief and Development Corporation, American Center for Law and Justice, The Flying Hospital, Inc., and several other organizations and broadcast entities.

CBN, founded in 1960, was the first Christian television network established in the United States. Today CBN is one of the world's largest television ministries and produces programming seen in 200 nations and heard in 70 languages including Russian, Arabic, Spanish, French, and Chinese. CBN's flagship program, *The 700 Club,* which Mr. Robertson hosts, can be seen in 97 percent of television markets across the United States and is one of the longest running religious television shows that reaches an average of one million American viewers daily.

Robertson was the founder and co-chairman of International Family Entertainment Inc. (IFE). Formed in 1990, IFE produced and distributed family entertainment and information programming worldwide. In 1997, IFE was sold to Fox. In 2001, Disney acquired the Fox Family Channel and named it ABC Family.

Robertson is the author of nineteen books. He and his wife Dede have four children and fourteen grandchildren and reside in Virginia Beach, Virginia.